A Note From Rick Renner

I am on a personal quest to see a "revival of the Bible" so people can establish their lives on a firm foundation that will stand strong and endure the test as end-time storm winds begin to intensify.

In order to experience a revival of the Bible in your personal life, it is important to take time each day to read, receive, and apply its truths to your life. James tells us that if we will continue in the perfect law of liberty — refusing to be forgetful hearers, but determined to be doers — we will be blessed in our ways. As you watch or listen to the programs in this series and work through this corresponding study guide, I trust you will search the Scriptures and allow the Holy Spirit to help you hear something new from God's Word that applies specifically to your life. I encourage you to be a doer of the Word He reveals to you. Whatever the cost, I assure you — it will be worth it.

> Thy words were found, and I did eat them;
> and thy word was unto me the joy and rejoicing of mine heart:
> for I am called by thy name, O Lord God of hosts.
> — Jeremiah 15:16

Your brother and friend in Jesus Christ,

Rick Renner

The Work of the Flesh vs. The Fruit of the Spirit

How To Use This Study Guide

This ten-lesson study guide corresponds to *"The Work of the Flesh vs. The Fruit of the Spirit" With Rick Renner* (**Renner TV**). Each lesson in this study guide covers a topic that is addressed during the program series, with questions and references supplied to draw you deeper into your own private study of the Scriptures on this subject.

To derive the most benefit from this study guide, consider the following:

First, watch or listen to the program prior to working through the corresponding lesson in this guide. (Programs can also be viewed at **renner.org** by clicking on the Media/Archives links.)

Second, take the time to look up the scriptures included in each lesson. Prayerfully consider their application to your own life.

Third, use a journal or notebook to make note of your answers to each lesson's Study Questions and Practical Application challenges.

Fourth, invest specific time in prayer and in the Word of God to consult with the Holy Spirit. Write down the scriptures or insights He reveals to you.

Finally, take action! Whatever the Lord tells you to do according to His Word, do it.

For added insights on this subject, it is recommended that you obtain Rick Renner's books *Sparkling Gems From the Greek, Volumes 1 and 2*. You may also select from Rick's other available resources by placing your order at **renner.org** or by calling 1-800-742-5593.

TOPIC

Walking in the Spirit

SCRIPTURES

1. **Galatians 5:15-17** — But if ye bite and devour one another, take heed that ye be not consumed one of another. This I say then, Walk in the Spirit, and ye shall not fulfil the lust of the flesh. For the flesh lusteth against the Spirit, and the Spirit against the flesh: and these are contrary the one to the other: so that ye cannot do the things that ye would.

GREEK WORDS

1. "bite" — **δάκνω** (*dakno*): to bite with the teeth; to wound with words; to lacerate and rend with insults and reproaches

2. "devour" — **κατεσθίω** (*katesthio*): from **κατά** (*kata*) and **ἐσθίω** (*esthio*); the word **κατά** (*kata*) means down, and **ἐσθίω** (*esthio*) means to eat or to consume; compounded, to eat, devour, gulp, or to swallow completely

3. "take heed" — **βλέπετε** (*blepete*): look, listen, take heed; intended to jolt the listener

4. "consumed" — **ἀναλίσκω** (*analisko*): consumed, eaten up, destroyed, devoured

5. "this I say" — **Λέγω δέ** (*Lego de*): I say categorically; I say emphatically

6. "walk" — **περιπατέω** (*peripateo*): a compound of the words **περι** (*peri*) and **πατέω** (*pateo*); the word **περι** (*peri*) means around and suggests the idea of something that is encircling; the word **πατέω** (*pateo*) means to walk and it denotes the movement of the feet; when compounded, to habitually walk around in one general vicinity; thus this word **περιπατέω** (*peripateo*) was often translated as the word 'live'

7. "shall not" — **οὐ μὴ** (*ou me*): the word **οὐ** (*ou*) is an emphatic no, with **μὴ** (*me*) which means no; you emphatically will not

8. "fulfil" — **τελέω** (*teleo*): to fulfill; to gratify; to satisfy

9. "lust" — ἐπιθυμία (*epithumia*): from ἐπί (*epi*) and θυμός (*thumos*); the word ἐπί (*epi*) means over and gives intensity to the word; the word θυμός (*thumos*) is passionate desire; when these words are compounded to form ἐπιθυμία (*epithumia*), it describes desire, cravings, or carnal longings of the flesh; one bent over and craving a thing

10. "flesh" — σαρκός (*sarkos*): flesh; carnal nature; base fleshly instincts

11. "lusteth" — ἐπιθυμία (*epithumia*): from ἐπί (*epi*) and θυμός (*thumos*); the word ἐπί (*epi*) means over and gives intensity to the word; the word θυμός (*thumos*) is passionate desire; when these words are compounded to form ἐπιθυμία (*epithumia*), it describes desire, cravings, or carnal longings of the flesh; one bent over and craving a thing

12. "against" — κατά (*kata*): down; against; conquer; dominate; squash

13. "the Spirit" — τοῦ Πνεύματος (*tou Pneumatos*): things of the Spirit

14. "and the Spirit" — τὸ δὲ Πνεῦμα (*to de Pneuma*): and categorically and emphatically the Spirit

15. "contrary" — ἀντίκειμαι (*antikeimai*): set in opposition against; strategically oppose; to take a stand against; completely unreconcilable, like two enemies on opposite sides of a war; an all-out war

SYNOPSIS

The ten lessons in this study on *The Work of the Flesh vs. The Fruit of the Spirit* will focus on the following topics:

- Walking in the Spirit
- The Works of the Flesh
- Adultery, Fornication, Uncleanness, Lasciviousness
- Idolatry, Witchcraft, Hatred, Variance, Emulations
- Wrath, Strife, Seditions, Heresies
- Envyings, Murders, Drunkenness, Revellings
- The Fruit of the Spirit
- The First Fruit
- Joy, Peace, Longsuffering, Gentleness
- Goodness, Faith, Meekness, Temperance

The emphasis of this lesson:

Walking in the Spirit means to live in the Spirit. It is a picture of one who has habitually walked and walked in a certain area for so long it has become second-nature. It is his realm and his environment. He knows the path so well that he can leisurely stroll on it blindfolded. This is the level of comfort and experience God wants us to have as we walk in the Spirit.

Have you ever wondered what it means to *walk in the Spirit*? That is what we are instructed to do in Galatians 5:16. Through the apostle Paul, God said, "…Walk in the Spirit, and ye shall not fulfill the lust of the flesh." In this lesson, we are going to dissect the meaning of this verse and learn how to experience a life of greater fulfillment and peace than ever before.

The Flesh Wants To 'Bite,' 'Devour,' and 'Consume'

In his letter to the Galatians, the apostle Paul wrote them to deal with their ungodly attitudes and actions toward one another. When word had reached him of the undercurrent of strife among the believers, he warned them, "But if ye bite and devour one another, take heed that ye be not consumed one of another."

There are several key words to understand in this verse, starting with the word "bite." In Greek, it is the word *dakno*, which literally means *to bite with the teeth*. Figuratively, it means *to wound with words* or *to lacerate and rend with insults and reproaches*. If you've ever found yourself in a heated conversation, you know how quickly your words can get out of control. With rising emotions often come wounding words — words we wish we could take back. But we can't. That is what happens when the flesh flares up and takes charge.

Next, Paul warned them not to "devour one another" (Galatians 5:15). The word "devour" is the Greek word *katesthio*, which is a compound of two words: the word *kata*, meaning *down*; and the word *esthio*, which means *to eat* or *to consume*. When these words are compounded, the new word *katesthio* means *to eat, devour, gulp, or to swallow completely*. Again, heated discussions can often make us feel like we've been chewed up or swallowed up by someone. That is exactly what the flesh wants to do — chew people up with its words.

That is why Paul said, "...Take heed that ye be not consumed one of another." In Greek, the words "take heed" are a translation of the word *blepete*, which is taken directly from the word *blepo*, and it means *to jolt and jar the listener* to sit up and really pay attention. The word *blepete* means *to look, listen,* or *take heed.*

Paul was trying to shake and wake his listeners, warning them that if they bite and devour one another with lacerating, wounding words they would be "consumed." This is the Greek word *analisko*, which means to be *totally consumed, eaten up, destroyed,* or *devoured.* That is what our flesh will do to others if we allow it to have its way.

The Alternative Is To 'Walk' in the Spirit

There is an alternative to the flesh biting, devouring, and consuming others, and the apostle Paul gives it to us in Galatians 5:16 where he declares, "This I say then, Walk in the Spirit, and ye shall not fulfil the lust of the flesh."

Notice that this verse opens with the words "this I say." It is a translation of the Greek phrase *Lego de*, which means *I say categorically* or *I say emphatically.* Again, Paul uses this phrase to really get the listener's attention and express an emphasis and urgency on what he is about to say.

Then he says, "...Walk in the Spirit..." (Galatians 5:16). This word "walk" is the Greek word *peripateo*, and it is a compound of the words *peri* and *pateo.* The word *peri* means *around* and suggests the idea of something that is *encircling.* The word *pateo* means *to walk* and it denotes *the movement of the feet.* When these words are compounded to form the word *peripateo*, it means *to habitually walk around in one general vicinity.* Thus this word *peripateo* was often translated as the word *'live.'*

This means that instead of being translated "walk in the Spirit," this phrase in Galatians 5:16 could be translated "live in the Spirit." This is a good rendering of the word *peripateo*, for indeed it suggests a person who has walked in one region for so long that it has now become his environment, his place of daily activity, and the sphere that encircles his existence.

One expositor notes the word *peripateo* could be explained by thinking of a person who has walked one path so habitually that he would be able to walk that path blindfolded because it is his path, his sphere, the place where he has habitually lived and functioned. He needs no help to walk there, because he knows that path. It is his path, his walk, his realm of life, and he feels very safe and comfortable there.

In the secular literature of Early New Testament times, the word *peripateo* often meant *to stroll*. In fact, many Greek scholars suggest that the best way to translate Galatians 5:16 is to "stroll in the Spirit." To stroll is to *take a leisurely walk*. A person who strolls is not an anxious, frustrated person who is fighting to do something or to get somewhere. A person who strolls is restful, relaxed, unhurried, peaceful, and calm. This wonderfully describes what it is like to walk in the Spirit.

When a person truly walks in the Spirit, the stress and anxieties of life are removed, and he or she moves into a realm where they can stroll along in continual rest, peace, and calmness. Therefore, the word *peripateo* — translated here as "walk" — suggests that one has walked and walked and walked in the Spirit for so long that it has become second-nature. It is a place of safety, security, and comfort. This is where God wants us to live — walking all the time in the Spirit.

When We Walk in the Spirit
We Avoid Gratifying Our Fleshly Cravings

Looking again at Paul's charge in Galatians 5:16, it says, "…Walk in the Spirit, and ye shall not fulfil the lust of the flesh." Notice the two words "shall not." They are a translation of the Greek phrase *ou me*. The word *ou* is *an emphatic no*, and the word *me* also means *no*. When *ou me* are joined together, it means *no, you emphatically will not*. Thus, Paul said, "When you walk in the Spirit, you emphatically will not in any way, no not ever, fulfil the lust of the flesh."

The word "fulfil" here is the Greek word *teleo*, which means *to fulfill*; *to gratify*; or *to satisfy*. It always carries the idea of *satisfying something* or *bringing something to completion*. With regard to walking in the Spirit, the Bible says we will never — no not ever — satisfy or gratify or bring to completion the lust of the flesh.

This brings us to the word "lust," which is the Greek word *epithumia*. It is a compound of the word *epi*, which means *over* and gives intensity to the word; and the word *thumos*, which describes *passionate desire*. When these words are compounded to form *epithumia*, it describes *desire, cravings, or carnal longings of the flesh.* Because the intensifying word *epi* is included, it is a picture of one bent over and craving a thing — much like a drug addict craves his next fix.

Specifically, Paul talks about the carnal cravings and longings of the "flesh." In Greek, this is the word *sarkos*, which describes *the flesh*; *carnal nature*; or *base, fleshly instincts.* The implication here is that our *flesh* has a will and mind of its own, and it wants *what* it wants *when* it wants it. If we let our flesh have its way, it will be bent over all the time, craving to do wrong things.

The Choice Is Ours

Basically, it all comes down to a *choice*: Are we going to give into our carnal, fleshly instincts and allow our flesh to satisfy and gratify its wrong cravings and desires. *Or* are we going to let the Holy Spirit who lives inside us control our lives. We are either going to be controlled by the Spirit or by our flesh.

Now, it's very important to realize that between our flesh and spirit is our *soul* — which is made up of our mind, our will, and our emotions. The soul is the deciding factor. With our mind and will, we choose who we're going to listen to — our *flesh* or the *Spirit.* If we choose to listen to our flesh and let our carnal instincts take the lead, we're going to produce some very negative, deathly results. But if we choose to walk in the Spirit, we will produce godly fruit that is very enjoyable for us and others.

The day we repent of our sins and surrender our lives to Jesus, He becomes our *Savior* and our *Lord.* When we call Jesus "Lord," we are submitting our soul — our mind, our will, and our emotions — to His leadership. As "Lord," He is the Supreme Master, and what He says goes. Our flesh doesn't get a vote. Therefore, when He commands us to "…Walk in the Spirit, and ye shall not fulfil the lust of the flesh" (Galatians 5:16), it is non-negotiable.

Taking into account the original Greek meaning of all the words we've studied, here is the *Renner Interpretive Version (RIV)* of Galatians 5:16:

> **Make the path of the Spirit the place where you habitually live and walk. Become so comfortable on this spiritual path that you learn to leisurely and peacefully stroll along in that realm. Living your life in this Spirit realm is the best way to guarantee**

that you will not allow the yearnings of your flesh to creep out and fulfill themselves.

It is time for you to do everything you can to move up into the higher realm of walking in the Spirit.

Your Flesh Wants To Dominate Your Life

The apostle Paul goes on to say, "For the flesh lusteth against the Spirit, and the Spirit against the flesh: and these are contrary the one to the other: so that ye cannot do the things that ye would" (Galatians 5:17). Once again we see the word "flesh," which is the Greek word *sarkos*, and it describes *the flesh*; *carnal nature*, or *base fleshly instincts*. The Bible says our *carnal nature* — our flesh — "lusteth against the Spirit."

This word "lusteth" is the Greek word *epithumia*, the same word translated as "lust" in Galatians 5:16. It is a compound of the word *epi*, which means *over* and is an intensifier; and the word *thumos*, which describes *passionate desire*. When these words are compounded to form *epithumia*, it describes *the desire, cravings, or carnal longings of the flesh*. And because the intensifying word *epi* is included, it is a picture of the flesh bent over and craving something — just like a drug addict craves his next fix.

Paul said, "For the flesh lusteth against the Spirit…" (Galatians 5:17). In Greek, the words "the Spirit" are *tou Pneumatos*, and it refers to *things of the Spirit*. The word "against" is the Greek word *kata*, and it describes *something coming down* or *something that is against*. It carries the idea of something that wants to *conquer, dominate,* or *squash*. The use of this word in the context of this verse lets us know the moment you begin to walk in the Spirit, your flesh will begin to wage war. It will fight against the Spirit fiercely to remain in control.

But the Spirit Is Fighting Against the Flesh

At the same time the flesh is fighting for supremacy, Paul said, "…and the Spirit [will fight] against the flesh…" (Galatians 5:17). This phrase in Greek literally says, "*And categorically and emphatically the Spirit against the flesh.*" The Holy Spirit living inside your spirit is diametrically opposed to your flesh dominating your life. The Spirit wants to rise up and take the driver's seat and crush your carnal nature. At the same time, the Spirit wants to cultivate the character of Christ in your life, which is why He is "against the flesh." Again, we see the word "against" — the Greek word *kata* — which depicts the Spirit's actions to *conquer*, to *dominate*, and to *squash* the flesh.

Paul said the flesh and Spirit are "…contrary the one to the other…" (Galatians 5:17). The word "contrary" here is the Greek word *antikeimai*. It is a compound of the word *anti*, meaning *against*, and the word *keimai*, meaning *to set* or *to position something*. When these words are compounded to form the word *antikeimai*, it means *to set in opposition against*, *to strategically oppose*; or *to take a stand against*. It depicts two enemies on opposite sides of a war that are completely irreconcilable.

Friend, the battle between your flesh and the Holy Spirit is an all-out war! Each one is fighting to gain and maintain the upper hand over the other. It is up to you to use your soul to choose who's in control of your life. That is why Paul emphatically urges you to "…Walk in the Spirit, and ye shall not fulfill the lust of the flesh" (Galatians 5:16).

Here once more is the *Renner Interpretive Version (RIV)* of Galatians 5:16:

> **Make the path of the Spirit the place where you habitually live and walk. Become so comfortable on this spiritual path that you learn to leisurely and peacefully stroll along in that realm. Living your life in this Spirit realm is the best way to guarantee that you will not allow the yearnings of your flesh to creep out and fulfill themselves.**

If you live your life walking in the Spirit, enjoyable fruit will be produced. But if you choose to give into the base instincts of your carnal nature, the outcome will be hard, laborious work, which we'll see more clearly in our next lesson.

STUDY QUESTIONS

Study to shew thyself approved unto God, a workman that needeth not to be ashamed, rightly dividing the word of truth.
— 2 Timothy 2:15

1. Prior to this lesson, what did you understand *walking in the Spirit* to mean? How has this teaching brought illumination and clarification?

2. Words are truly powerful, but what they produce is determined by whether they are spoken in the flesh or by the Spirit. Take a few moments to look up these Scripture verses and write down what the

Lord reveals to you about the power released through the words of your lips.

- Proverbs 18:20,21
- Psalm 37:30,31; Proverbs 10:11,21,31,32 (mouth of righteous brings wisdom)
- Proverbs 10:19; 13:3; 21:23

PRACTICAL APPLICATION

But be ye doers of the word, and not hearers only,
deceiving your own selves.
—James 1:22

1. Using your own words, what would you say it means to *walk in the Spirit*?
2. Have you ever been wounded by someone else's words? Did their cutting remarks leave you lacerated in your soul? Did you feel as though you were swallowed up by accusations that weren't true? How did you respond? If you've never taken time to ask God to heal your wounded soul, do it now.
3. In what ways have you personally experienced the joy of walking in the Spirit? Are there any areas of your life where you have intentionally or unintentionally allowed your flesh to remain in control over you? If so, where, and what can you do to bring these things under the leadership of the Holy Spirit?

LESSON 2

TOPIC

The Works of the Flesh

SCRIPTURES

1. **Galatians 5:15-17,19-21** — But if ye bite and devour one another, take heed that ye be not consumed one of another. This I say then, Walk in the Spirit, and ye shall not fulfil the lust of the flesh. For the flesh lusteth against the Spirit, and the Spirit against the flesh:

and these are contrary the one to the other: so that ye cannot do the things that ye would. …Now the works of the flesh are manifest, which are these; Adultery, fornication, uncleanness, lasciviousness, idolatry, witchcraft, hatred, variance, emulations, wrath, strife, seditions, heresies, envyings, murders, drunkenness, revellings, and such like.…

GREEK WORDS

1. "bite" — **δάκνω** (*dakno*): to bite with the teeth; to wound with words; to lacerate and rend with insults and reproaches

2. "devour" — **κατεσθίω** (*katesthio*): from **κατά** (*kata*) and **ἐσθίω** (*esthio*); the word **κατά** (*kata*) means down, and **ἐσθίω** (*esthio*): means to eat or to consume; compounded, to eat, devour, gulp, or to swallow completely

3. "take heed" — **βλέπετε** (*blepete*): look, listen, take heed; intended to jolt the listener

4. "consumed" — **ἀναλίσκω** (*analisko*): consumed, eaten up, destroyed, devoured

5. "this I say" — **Λέγω δέ** (*Lego de*): I say categorically; I say emphatically

6. "walk" — **περιπατέω** (*peripateo*): a compound of the words **περι** (*peri*) and **πατέω** (*pateo*); the word **περι** (*peri*) means around and suggests the idea of something that is encircling; the word **πατέω** (*pateo*) means to walk and it denotes the movement of the feet; when compounded, to habitually walk around in one general vicinity; thus this word **περιπατέω** (*peripateo*) was often translated as the word 'live'

7. "shall not" — **οὐ μὴ** (*ou me*): the word **οὐ** (*ou*) is an emphatic no, with **μὴ** (*me*) which means no; you emphatically will not

8. "fulfil" — **τελέω** (*teleo*): to fulfill; to gratify; to satisfy

9. "lust" — **ἐπιθυμία** (*epithumia*): from **ἐπί** (*epi*) and **θυμός** (*thumos*); the word **ἐπί** (*epi*) means over and gives intensity to the word; the word **θυμός** (*thumos*) is passionate desire; when these words are compounded to form **ἐπιθυμία** (*epithumia*), it describes desire, cravings, or carnal longings of the flesh; one bent over and craving a thing

10. "flesh" — **σαρκός** (*sarkos*): flesh; carnal nature; base fleshly instincts

11. "the Spirit" — **τοῦ Πνεύματος** (*tou Pneumatos*): things of the Spirit

12. "and the Spirit" — **τὸ δὲ Πνεῦμα** (*to de Pneuma*): and categorically and emphatically the Spirit

13. "against" — **κατά** (*kata*): down; against; conquer; dominate; squash

14. "contrary" — **ἀντίκειμαι** (*antikeimai*): set in opposition against; strategically oppose; to take a stand against; completely unreconcilable, like two enemies on opposite sides of a war; an all-out war

15. "works" — **ἔργα** (*erga*): labor or hard work; signifies some kind of action, deed, or activity; very often referred to a person's occupation, to one's labor, or to the things produced by someone's effort or life; describes a person's line of work, his career, his labor, or his profession; denotes the results of hard work

16. "manifest" — **φανερός** (*phaneros*): to appear, to manifest, to become visible, to become apparent, to become seen, to be well known, or to become conspicuous

SYNOPSIS

All throughout the New Testament, the Bible talks about the flesh — also known as our carnal nature. The apostle Paul — who was a pillar of the Early Church — knew the frustrations of dealing with the flesh. He devoted a great deal of Romans 6 and 7 talking about it. In the midst of his writing, he declared, "For I know that nothing good dwells in me, that is, in my flesh. For I have the desire to do what is right, but not the ability to carry it out" (Romans 7:18 *ESV*).

Indeed, there is nothing good in our flesh. When we let it control our lives, it only produces death and decay. Thankfully, we don't have to live our lives dominated by our flesh. We can choose to walk in the Spirit and experience the blessed, life-giving fruit He produces in and through us.

The emphasis of this lesson:

The work of the flesh is hard, exhausting work. When we allow our carnal nature to run our lives, the results we can expect to receive from our efforts are adultery, fornication, uncleanness, lasciviousness, idolatry, witchcraft, hatred, variance, emulations, wrath, strife, seditions, heresies, envyings, murders, drunkenness, and revellings.

A REVIEW OF LESSON 1

Verbal Assassination Is the Flesh's Aspiration

As we saw in our first lesson, the apostle Paul wrote to believers in Galatia in order to correct their ungodly attitudes and actions toward one another. Apparently, a number of the people were giving into their old, fleshly nature and beginning to treat each other horribly. He addressed them by saying, "But if ye bite and devour one another, take heed that ye be not consumed one of another" (Galatians 5:15).

We noted that the word "bite" is the Greek word *dakno*, which literally means *to bite with the teeth*. Figuratively, it means *to wound with words* or *to lacerate and rend with insults and reproaches*. When we give into the flesh in a heated conversation, our words can quickly get out of control. When emotions escalate, wounding words begin to fly — words we wish we could take back. But we can't. That's what happens when the flesh flares up and takes charge.

If we continue to operate in the flesh, the Bible says we will begin to "devour" each other. This word "devour" is the Greek word *katesthio*, which is a compound of the words *kata* and *esthio*. The word *kata* means *down*, and the word *esthio*, means *to eat* or *to consume*. When these words are joined, the new word *katesthio* means *to eat, devour, gulp, or to swallow completely*. That is exactly what the flesh wants to do — devour other people with devastatingly harsh words.

With great urgency, Paul said, "…Take heed that ye be not consumed one of another" (Galatians 5:15). In Greek, the phrase "take heed" is the word *blepete*, which is derived directly from the word *blepo*, a term used to jolt and jar the listener to sit up and really pay attention. This word *blepete* means *to look, listen,* or *take heed*.

Paul was trying to shake and wake his listeners to put a stop to biting and devouring one another with lacerating, wounding words. Otherwise, they would be "consumed." This is the Greek word *analisko*, and it means to be *totally consumed, eaten up, destroyed,* or *devoured*. That is what our crazy flesh will do to others if we allow it to have its way.

God Commands Us To 'Walk in the Spirit'

Thank God, through faith in the finished work of Jesus Christ, we have an alternative. Instead of biting, devouring, and consuming one another, the apostle Paul said, "This I say then, Walk in the Spirit, and ye shall not fulfil the lust of the flesh" (Galatians 5:16).

The opening phrase — "this I say" — is a translation of the Greek words *Lego de*, which mean *I say categorically* or *I say emphatically*. Here Paul is lifting up his voice and giving the command for us as believers to rise up and take the higher road of *walking in the Spirit*. And this is not to be an occasional exercise. Rather, it is to be an ongoing way of life.

That is what the word "walk" means in Galatians 5:16. It is the Greek word *peripateo*, which is a compound of the words *peri* and *pateo*. The word *peri* means *around* and indicates something that is *encircling*. The word *pateo* means *to walk a path* and it denotes *the movement of the feet*. When these words are compounded to form the word *peripateo*, it literally means *to habitually walk around in one general vicinity all the time*. Hence, this word *peripateo* was often translated as the word '*live.*'

So "walking in the Spirit" is not a hit-or-miss activity we do every now and then. When Paul says, "Walk in the Spirit," it would better be translated as, "Live in the Spirit." The original Greek here depicts a person who has walked in one region for so long that it has now become his environment, his place of daily activity, and the sphere that encircles his existence.

One expositor has stated that the word *peripateo* is a picture of a person who has habitually walked one path for so long that now he could walk it blindfolded because it is his path, his sphere, his realm of life, the place where he has consistently lived and functioned. He needs no help to walk there, because he knows that path and feels very safe and comfortable there.

In the secular literature of Early New Testament times, the word *peripateo* often meant *to stroll*. To stroll is to *take a leisurely walk*. A person who strolls is not an anxious, frustrated person who is fighting to do something or to get somewhere. A person who strolls is restful, relaxed, unhurried, peaceful, and calm. This is a perfect picture of what it means to *walk in the Spirit*.

When we walk in the Spirit, the stress and anxieties of life are removed, and we move into a realm where we can stroll along in continual rest, peace, and calmness. God wants us to become so familiar with habitually walking (*peripateo*) in the Spirit that it becomes second-nature. It is a place of great safety, security, and comfort where God wants us to live.

When We Walk in the Spirit We Avoid Gratifying Our Fleshly Cravings

It's important to see that Paul said when you walk in the Spirit, "…Ye shall not fulfil the lust of the flesh" (Galatians 5:16). The words "shall not" here are a translation of the Greek phrase *ou me*. The word *ou* is *an emphatic no*, and the word *me* is a negating or canceling word. When *ou me* are joined, it is the equivalent of saying, "*No, in no way, you will emphatically not.*" Inserting this meaning into Galatians 5:17, it says, "When you walk in the Spirit, you will emphatically not in any way, no not ever, fulfil the lust of the flesh."

The word "fulfil" here is the Greek word *teleo*, which means *to fulfill; to gratify*; or *to satisfy*, and it always carries the idea of *taking something from an embryonic stage to full development*. The implication here is that the flesh always wants to satisfy its cravings until that expression of carnality is fully developed. But if we choose to walk in the Spirit, we will put a halt to that fleshly development.

Specifically, we will put a stop to the "lust of the flesh." In Greek, the word for "lust" is *epithumia*. It is a compound of the words *epi* and *thumos*. The word *epi* means *over* and gives intensity to the word; and the word *thumos* describes *passionate desire*. When these words are compounded to form *epithumia*, it describes *desire, cravings, or carnal longings of the flesh*. It pictures someone yearning and craving something so desperately he is bent over in desire for it.

Paul says these carnal cravings and longings are of the "flesh." In Greek, this is the word *sarkos*, which describes *the flesh*; *carnal nature*; or *base fleshly instincts*. This tells us that our flesh has a mind and will of its own, and if we don't put it to death by the power of the Holy Spirit, it will wreak havoc in our lives, producing a bumper crop of rotten fruit.

Your Soul Is the Deciding Factor

Each of us has a choice: We are either going to give into our carnal instincts and allow our flesh to satisfy and gratify its wrong cravings, *or* we're going to let the Holy Spirit who lives inside us control our lives. We cannot walk in the Spirit and follow our flesh simultaneously.

You are a three-part being. You are a spirit, you have a soul, and you live in a body. Between your spirit and your body (flesh) is your soul, which is made up of your mind, will, and emotions. The soul is the control center of your life. It is the deciding factor. With your mind and will, you choose what part of you is going to lead your life — your flesh or your spirit. If you choose to listen to your flesh, your carnal instincts will be empowered to produce very negative results. But if you choose to walk in the Spirit, you will produce godly fruit that is very enjoyable.

If you have been walking in the flesh for a long time, you will naturally and almost effortlessly gravitate toward fulfilling your fleshly, base desires. To break free from this deadly pattern, you must learn to crucify your flesh by the power of the Holy Spirit. This is a daily — sometimes moment-by-moment — decision to say *yes* to the Holy Spirit and *no* to what your flesh is demanding. Your soul — your mind and will — make this choice.

Taking into account the original Greek meaning of all the words we've studied, here is the *Renner Interpretive Version (RIV)* of Galatians 5:16:

> **Make the path of the Spirit the place where you habitually live and walk. Become so comfortable on this spiritual path that you learn to leisurely and peacefully stroll along in that realm. Living your life in this Spirit realm is the best way to guarantee that you will not allow the yearnings of your flesh to creep out and fulfill themselves.**

When you choose to walk in the Spirit, you effectively pull the plug on the power of the flesh.

It's an All-Out War

In Galatians 5:17, the apostle Paul went on to say, "For the flesh lusteth against the Spirit, and the Spirit against the flesh: and these are contrary the one to the other: so that ye cannot do the things that ye would." Once more we see the word "flesh" — the Greek word *sarkos* — and it describes *the flesh*; *carnal nature*; or *base fleshly instincts*. The Bible says our flesh "lusteth against the Spirit."

The word "against" here is the Greek word *kata*, which means *down, against, conquer, dominate*, or *squash*. The use of this word in the context of this verse lets us know the moment you begin to walk in the Spirit, your flesh will declare war against the Spirit, attempting to dominate, conquer, and squash every effort to walk in godliness. It will do its best to pull you down and back under its carnal control.

Why the war? Paul said the flesh and Spirit are "contrary" to one another. This word "contrary" is the Greek word *antikeimai*, which is a compound of the word *anti*, meaning *against*, and the word *keimai*, meaning *to set* or *to position something*. When these words are joined to form the word *antikeimai*, it means *to set in opposition against*; *to strategically oppose*; or *to take a stand against*. It depicts two enemies on opposite sides of a war that are completely irreconcilable; it is the picture of an all-out war.

This lets you know that when you choose to walk in the Spirit, don't be surprised if your flesh throws a fit. It is in an all-out war with the Spirit, and it will do everything within its power to remain in control.

The Flesh Produces 'Works'

The apostle Paul continued in Galatians 5:19 when he wrote, "Now the works of the flesh are manifest…." The word "works" in this verse is the Greek word *erga*, which describes *labor* or *hard work*. Thus, when the "flesh" — *the carnal nature or base fleshly instincts* — is in control it yields *labor* or *hard work*. This is vastly different from what happens when the Spirit is in control. It produces good fruit.

The word "works" — the Greek word *erga* — signifies some kind of *action, deed*, or *activity*. Very often it referred to *a person's occupation, to one's labor*, or *to the things produced by someone's effort or life*. It can describe a person's line of work, his career, or his profession. Essentially, it denotes the results of hard work.

The Bible states, "Now the works of the flesh are *manifest*…" (Galatians 5:19). The word "manifest" in Greek is the word *phaneros*, which means *to appear, to manifest, to become visible, to become apparent, to become seen, to be well known*, or *to become conspicuous*. What are the results of the flesh's hard work? Paul lists them in Galatians 5:19-21:

Now the works of the flesh are manifest, which are these; adultery, fornication, uncleanness, lasciviousness, idolatry, witchcraft, hatred, variance, emulations, wrath, strife, seditions, heresies, envyings, murders, drunkenness, revellings, and such like...

When we let our "flesh" — the Greek word *sarkos*, describing the *carnal nature* — run our lives, these are the kinds of byproducts we can expect to have.

But that doesn't have to be your experience. You can follow God's instruction through Paul in Galatians 5:16: "This I say then, Walk in the Spirit, and ye shall not fulfil the lust of the flesh."

Again, taking into account the original Greek meaning of the words we've examined, here is the *Renner Interpretive Version (RIV)* of Galatians 5:16:

Make the path of the Spirit the place where you habitually live and walk. Become so comfortable on this spiritual path that you learn to leisurely and peacefully stroll along in that realm. Living your life in this Spirit realm is the best way to guarantee that you will not allow the yearnings of your flesh to creep out and fulfill themselves.

In our next lesson, we will take a closer look at the meaning of the first four works of the flesh: *adultery, fornication, uncleanness,* and *lasciviousness*.

STUDY QUESTIONS

> Study to shew thyself approved unto God, a workman that needeth
> not to be ashamed, rightly dividing the word of truth.
> — 2 Timothy 2:15

1. When it comes to walking in the Spirit and *not* fulfilling the lust of the flesh, how important do you think *Bible reading* and *prayer* are? Consider what God says in Second Timothy 3:15-17, Hebrews 4:12; and James 1:21-25 as you answer.

2. You are a three-part being created in God's image. You are a *spirit*, you have a *soul*, and you live in a *body*. Although your spirit is immediately made perfect the moment you're born again, your soul is renewed *progressively* throughout your life. What does First Thessalonians

5:23 and 24 say about this process called *sanctification*? (Also consider Second Corinthians 3:17,18; Philippians 1:6; Jude 24.)

PRACTICAL APPLICATION

> But be ye doers of the word, and not hearers only,
> deceiving your own selves.
> —James 1:22

1. The word "flesh" describes *one's carnal nature* or *base fleshly instincts*. What fleshly cravings have you struggled with most in your life? Are you giving into your flesh *less* now than a year ago? How about five years ago? What seems to help you avoid giving in to these ungodly longings?

2. If Jesus were to evaluate your life to verify what percentage of your time is lived in the *Spirit* and what portion is lived in the *flesh*, what do you think He would discover?

3. Take a few moments to pray: *Lord, what can I do to make the path of the Holy Spirit the place where I habitually live and walk? How can I become so comfortable living in the Spirit that I no longer allow the cravings of my flesh to rule my life?* Be still and listen. What is the Holy Spirit speaking to you?

LESSON 3

TOPIC

Adultery, Fornication, Uncleanness, Lasciviousness

SCRIPTURES

1. **Galatians 5:16** — This I say then, Walk in the Spirit, and ye shall not fulfil the lust of the flesh.

2. **Galatians 5:19-21** — Now the works of the flesh are manifest, which are these; Adultery, fornication, uncleanness, lasciviousness, idolatry, witchcraft, hatred, variance, emulations, wrath, strife, seditions, heresies, envyings, murders, drunkenness, revellings, and such like....

3. **Matthew 5:28** — But I say unto you, That whosoever looketh on a woman to lust after her hath committed adultery with her already in his heart.

4. **Mark 1:23** — And there was in their synagogue a man with an unclean spirit....

5. **Mark 5:2** — And when he was come out of the ship, immediately there met him out of the tombs a man with an unclean spirit.

6. **Romans 6:16** — Know ye not, that to whom ye yield yourselves servants to obey, his servants ye are to whom ye obey....

GREEK WORDS

1. "this I say" — **Λέγω δέ** (*Lego de*): I say categorically; I say emphatically

2. "walk" — **περιπατέω** (*peripateo*): a compound of the words **περι** (*peri*) and **πατέω** (*pateo*); the word **περι** (*peri*) means around and suggests the idea of something that is encircling; the word **πατέω** (*pateo*) means to walk and it denotes the movement of the feet; when compounded, to habitually walk around in one general vicinity; thus this word **περιπατέω** (*peripateo*) was often translated as the word 'live'

3. "shall not" — **οὐ μὴ** (*ou me*): the word **οὐ** (*ou*) is an emphatic no, with **μὴ** (*me*) which means no; you emphatically will not

4. "fulfil" — **τελέω** (*teleo*): to fulfill; to gratify; to satisfy

5. "lust" — **ἐπιθυμία** (*epithumia*): from **ἐπί** (*epi*) and **θυμός** (*thumos*); the word **ἐπί** (*epi*) means over and gives intensity to the word; the word **θυμός** (*thumos*) is passionate desire; when these words are compounded to form **ἐπιθυμία** (*epithumia*), it describes desire, cravings, or carnal longings of the flesh; one bent over and craving a thing

6. "flesh" — **σαρκός** (*sarkos*): flesh; carnal nature; base fleshly instincts

7. "works" — **ἔργα** (*erga*): labor or hard work

8. "manifest" — **φανερός** (*phaneros*): to appear, to manifest, to become visible, to become apparent, to become seen, to be well known, or to become conspicuous

9. "adultery" and "fornication" — **πορνεία** (*porneia*): it includes all sexual activity outside of marriage, including adultery and homosexuality

10. "uncleanness" — **ἀκαθαρσία** (*akatharsia*): the word **καθαίρω** (*kathairo*) with the prefix **ἀ** (*a*) added; the word **καθαίρω** (*kathairo*) means cleansed or pure, but when **ἀ** (*a*) is added, the condition is reversed, making the object dirty or unclean; in the New Testament, it refers

to lewd or unclean thoughts that eventually produce lewd or unclean actions

11. "lasciviousness" — ἀσέλγεια (*aselgeia*): excess; primarily refers to the excessive consumption of food or wild, undisciplined living that is especially marked by unbridled sex; ἀσέλγεια (*aselgeia*) is listed as the principal sin of the cities of Sodom and Gomorrah (see 2 Peter 2:6) and the reason that God overthrew them

SYNOPSIS

Choices — they are always before us. Right choices lead to right results, and wrong choices lead to wrong results. Through Moses, God declared this eternal truth: "I call heaven and earth as witnesses today against you, that I have set before you life and death, blessing and cursing; therefore *choose life*, that both you and your descendants may live" (Deuteronomy 30:19 *NKJV*).

One recurring choice we all have to make is whether we will walk in the Spirit or give into the cravings of our carnal nature. If we choose to walk after the flesh, it will yield death-permeated works. But if we choose to walk in the Spirit, the Spirit will produce supernatural, life-giving fruit. In this lesson, we will focus our attention on the meaning of the first four works of the flesh: *adultery*, *fornication*, *uncleanness*, and *lasciviousness*.

The emphasis of this lesson:

In the original Greek text of Scripture, adultery and fornication are from the same word, and it describes all sexual activity outside of marriage. Uncleanness is lewd or unclean thoughts that eventually produce lewd or unclean actions. And lasciviousness refers to the excessive consumption of food or wild, undisciplined living that's especially marked by unbridled sex.

A REVIEW OF OUR ANCHOR VERSE

Galatians 5:16

We Are To 'Walk in the Spirit'

Speaking to the believers in Galatia — and in all generations — the apostle Paul issued this command: "This I say then, Walk in the Spirit, and ye shall not fulfil the lust of the flesh" (Galatians 5:16). When Paul said, "This I say," he used the Greek words *Lego de*. *Lego* means *I say*, but the word *de* is emphatic and categorical. The use of these words together indicates he was raising his voice to get everyone's attention. It is as if he was saying, "Hey, I'm telling you emphatically and I'm telling you categorically that if you walk in the Spirit, you will not fulfill the lust of the flesh."

We have noted that the word "walk" in this verse is the Greek word *peripateo*, which is a compound of the words *peri* and *pateo*. The word *peri* means *around* and indicates something that is *encircling*, and the word *pateo* comes from the Greek word for *a path*. When these words are compounded to form the word *peripateo*, it literally means *to habitually walk around in one general vicinity all the time*. It is the picture of someone who has walked and walked on a certain path for so long it has become like home to them.

So "walking in the Spirit" is not a hit-or-miss activity we do every once in a while. It is a way of life. The original Greek here depicts a person who has walked in one region for so long that it has now become his environment, his place of daily activity, and the sphere that encircles his existence. Thus, the command to "walk in the Spirit" could better be translated as "live in the Spirit."

And We Shall Not Fulfill the Lust of the Flesh

Paul said when you walk in the Spirit, "…Ye shall not fulfil the lust of the flesh" (Galatians 5:16). The phrase "shall not" is a translation of the Greek words *ou me*. The word *ou* means *emphatically no*, and the word *me* also means *no*. When *ou me* are joined, it means *no, you absolutely will not*. This is God's guarantee that you cannot and will not walk in the flesh if you choose the path of life in the Spirit. It is the equivalent of Paul saying, "When you walk in the Spirit, you emphatically will not in any way, no not ever, fulfill the lust of the flesh."

The word "fulfil" here is the Greek word *teleo*, which means *to fulfill*; *to gratify*; or *to satisfy*. It always describes *something that grows up and reaches full maturity*. It is something that started out in an infant stage and finally matured and became fully developed. Therefore, in the context of this verse, Paul is saying, "When you habitually live in the Spirit, you will put a stop to the development of the works of the flesh and sin in your life."

This brings us to the word "lust" — the Greek word *epithumia*. It is a compound of the word *epi*, which means *over* and gives the word intensity; and the word *thumos*, which describes *passionate desire*. When these words are compounded to form *epithumia*, it describes *desire, cravings, or carnal longings of the flesh*. Because the intensifying word *epi* is included, it is a picture of one bent over and craving and yearning for something.

Paul specifies that *lust* is of the "flesh." In Greek, "flesh" is the word *sarkos*, and it describes *the flesh*; *carnal cravings*; or *sinful impulses*. Ephesians 2:3 says the flesh has desires, lusts, and a mind of its own. If you don't crucify it and keep it under control, it will manifest its evil fruits. In other words, the flesh will go to work and begin producing all kinds of deadly results.

Taking into account the original Greek meaning of the key words in this verse, here is the *Renner Interpretive Version (RIV)* of Galatians 5:16:

> **Make the path of the Spirit the place where you habitually live and walk. Become so comfortable on this spiritual path that you learn to leisurely and peacefully stroll along in that realm. Living your life in this Spirit realm is the best way to guarantee that you will not allow the yearnings of your flesh to creep out and fulfill themselves.**

The Flesh Produces Hard 'Works'

The apostle Paul went on to write, "Now the works of the flesh are manifest..." (Galatians 5:19). The word "works" here is the Greek word *erga*, which describes *labor* or *hard work*. It signifies some kind of *action, deed,* or *activity* and often refers to *a person's occupation, to one's labor,* or *to the things produced by someone's effort or life*. What the flesh produces is *hard, laborious work*.

Indeed, a life dominated by the flesh is a *hard life*. It is filled with excess, imbalance, laziness, self-abuse, hatred, strife, bitterness, irresponsibility, and neglect. The way of the flesh is the hardest route for any individual to take. But unless you take your flesh to the Cross and mortify it by the power of the Holy Spirit, it will go to work and manifest its evil fruits! It will keep screaming for you to surrender to it and allow it to produce its ruinous effects in your life.

The Bible states, "Now the works of the flesh are *manifest*..." (Galatians 5:19). The word "manifest" in Greek is the word *phaneros*, and it means *to appear, to manifest, to become visible, to become apparent, to become seen, to be well known,* or *to become conspicuous.* Again, if you don't crucify your flesh — and keep it under control — the negative, disastrous consequences will become visibly apparent to you and everyone else.

Galatians 5:19-21 lists 17 works of the flesh: "...Adultery, fornication, uncleanness, lasciviousness, idolatry, witchcraft, hatred, variance, emulations, wrath, strife, seditions, heresies, envyings, murders, drunkenness, revellings, and such like...." The first four works included in this passage are *adultery, fornication, uncleanness,* and *lasciviousness,* and they are all sexual sins.

We live in a day when moral standards have deteriorated drastically. Things that were once considered sinful and shameful a generation ago are now practiced and even celebrated in a widespread manner — even in the Church. Although many people may have changed what they think about sexual sin, God has not. He is the same yesterday, today, and forever (*see* Hebrews 13:8). What He defined as sin in Scripture thousands of years ago is still defined as sin by Him today.

Let's take a closer look at the meaning of these first four sexual sins.

Adultery and Fornication
Are Expressions of the Same Root Sin

In the *King James Version* of Galatians 5:19, Paul begins his list of the works of the flesh with the sexual sins of "adultery" and "fornication." In Greek, however, the words "adultery" and "fornication" come from the same word, and that word is *porneia.* This Greek term includes *all sexual activity outside of marriage* — including adultery and homosexuality

When referring to *a woman who committed adultery*, the New Testament uses the word *pornos.* It is the word for *a prostitute,* and it describes *a woman who has committed adultery and has prostituted herself.* She may not have sold herself for money. Nevertheless, she traded a part of herself

— perhaps her heart, her emotions, or her body — for romance, emotional support, or for a variety of other things. Regardless of why, God says she has sold herself and entered into prostitution.

Don't deceive yourself into thinking that the word *pornos* only refers to a woman who professionally prostitutes herself by walking the streets at night or working in an escort service. This word *pornos* describes any woman who has committed adultery. It leaves no room for doubt that in God's view, any woman who has sold some or all of herself in exchange for something from someone has fallen into the sin of prostitution. One may try to give reasons or excuses to explain why an illicit relationship occurred, but God views such a relationship as an act of prostitution.

When referring to *a man who committed adultery*, the New Testament uses the word *porneia*. This word depicts *a man who has had sexual intercourse with a prostitute*. Any time a man has sexual relations with a woman who is not his wife, God says his actions are equivalent to sleeping with a prostitute. Although his emotions may try to tell him that he has found the sweetheart of his dreams or put a different light on what took place, that is not how God sees it. The Greek word *porneia* means he has slept with a prostitute.

It must be noted that the word "pornography" comes from this same Greek word *porneia*. It is a compound of the Greek word *pornos* — the same word used above for *an adulteress* or *a prostitute* — and the word *grapho*, which means *to write*. When these two words are compounded to form *pornography*, it refers to *the writings* or *reflections about prostitution*. This means when a person meditates on the writings or photography contained in pornography, it is the equivalent of committing *mental prostitution*.

This sheds eye-opening new light on what Jesus said in Matthew 5:28: "But I say unto you, That whosoever looketh on a woman to lust after her hath committed adultery with her already in his heart."

Altogether, what you have just read in this section is the actual meaning of the Greek word "adultery" that is used throughout the New Testament. Again, in the original Greek, adultery and fornication are both encapsulated in the word *porneia*. It is an all-inclusive word that includes all forms of sexual activity outside of marriage.

Uncleanness Is Directly Linked to Lewd Thinking

The third work of the flesh listed in Galatians 5:19 is "uncleanness," from the Greek word *akatharsia* — which is the word *kathairo* with the prefix *a* added. The word *kathairo* means *cleansed* or *pure*, but when *a* is added to the front, the condition is reversed, making the object *dirty* or *unclean*. In the New Testament, it refers to *lewd or unclean thoughts that eventually produce lewd or unclean actions.*

As used in the Gospels and Paul's epistles, there is a strong suggestion that these actions begin in the mind as unclean thoughts before they manifest as unclean deeds. One example of its use is found in Mark 1:23, which says, "And there was in their synagogue a man with an unclean spirit...." The original Greek text actually says that this man was *"gripped by the control of an unclean spirit."* It seems this man had pondered on *lewd thoughts* for so long that he had thrown open the door for these thoughts to seize and control him. Eventually, he found himself "in the grip" or "in the clutch" of an unclean spirit.

The word *akatharsia* makes one wonder whether or not this demon found entrance into this man's life because he allowed his mind to dwell on things that were unclean. Had he committed *mental prostitution* to such an extent that it opened the door for him to be completely controlled by spirits of uncleanness? The Bible doesn't say exactly so, but the use of this word makes this a possibility.

In Mark 5:2, we find another example of a man with an unclean spirit. The Bible says, "And when he [Jesus] was come out of the ship, immediately there met him out of the tombs a man with an unclean spirit." The word "unclean" here is also the word *akatharsia*. Just as in Mark 1:23, this man in Mark 5:2 — the demoniac of Gadara — was "in the grip" or "in the clutch" of an unclean spirit.

Did Satan lure these two men into pornography of some kind or into unclean thoughts or into fornication and then begin to build a stronghold of uncleanness in their minds that was so robust he was able to completely control them? Whatever the case, the use of the word *akatharsia* pictures individuals whose condition seems to have begun with *impure, lewd, dirty thoughts.*

Never forget what Paul told us in Romans 6:16: "Know ye not, that to whom ye yield yourselves servants to obey, his servants ye are to whom ye obey; whether of sin unto death, or of obedience unto righteousness."

Whatever you give your mind to eventually becomes your master. Was this the case with these two demon-possessed men in Mark 1:23 and Mark 5:2? It would surely seem so. This should certainly make us want to take charge of our thought life and not allow uncleanness to have any place in our minds!

Lasciviousness Describes Excessiveness in Two Primary Areas

The next sin listed in the series of the works of the flesh is "lasciviousness." It is the Greek word *aselgeia*, which describes *excess*. Interestingly, it primarily refers to *the excessive consumption of food* or *wild, undisciplined living that is especially marked by unbridled sex*. This word *aselgeia* — translated here as "lasciviousness" — is listed as the principal sin of the cities of Sodom and Gomorrah (*see* 2 Peter 2:6) and the reason that God overthrew them.

Again, it must be noted that the word *aselgeia* (lasciviousness) also refers to *the excessive consumption of food*. This means that in God's mind, it is just as perverted to overindulge in food as it is to engage in sinful sexual activities! This should certainly change the way all of us see overeating.

If you have fallen into any of these works of the flesh, ask the Holy Spirit to open your eyes to see these sins as He sees them. Once you get a revelation of His perspective, you'll understand the grossness of fleshly activity in God's sight and you will want to be changed!

If you confess your sin to God, He will forgive you — and then you can move on with life. If your actions have violated your spouse or anyone else, pray for God's grace to be upon them to forgive you as you honestly share with them what you have struggled with.

In our next lesson, we will unpack the meaning of five additional works of the flesh that are listed in Galatians 5:20. They are *idolatry, witchcraft, hatred, variance,* and *emulations*.

STUDY QUESTIONS

Study to shew thyself approved unto God, a workman that needeth
not to be ashamed, rightly dividing the word of truth.
— 2 Timothy 2:15

1. There are many sins a person can fall into and even practice. But sex-
    ual sin is in a class by itself. What does the Holy Spirit speak through
    Paul in First Corinthians 6:12-20 about the infectious influence of
    sexual sin? What makes it different than other sins, and how does
    God want you to handle it? (Also consider First Thessalonians 4:3-8
    as you answer.)

2. In the Bible, the Greek word *porneia* is the all-inclusive word used to
    describe all forms of sexual activity outside of marriage. That said, how
    does this affect your view of someone who has committed adultery?
    What about someone involved in homosexuality or lesbianism? And
    how does this affect your view of pornography?

3. One of the works of the flesh is called "lasciviousness," which is the
    Greek word *aselgeia*. In addition to describing a wild, undisciplined
    life of unbridled sex, it also refers to *the excessive consumption of food*.
    This means that in God's mind, it is just as perverted to overindulge
    in food as it is to engage in sinful sexual activities. So how does this
    make you feel about *overeating*?

PRACTICAL APPLICATION

But be ye doers of the word, and not hearers only,
deceiving your own selves.
— James 1:22

1. For some believers sexual sin is not a problem — but overeating is.
    Has this been an area where you've struggled? Now that you know
    overeating and gluttony are one of the works of the flesh, what prac-
    tical steps do you need to begin taking to break free from this sin that
    hurts you and is offensive to God?

2. If you have fallen into any of these works of the flesh, pray and ask the
    Holy Spirit to open your eyes to see these sins as He sees them. Then
    repent and ask God to forgive you and cleanse you from all unrigh-
    teousness. (Consider David's prayer in Psalm 51:1-12 after he fell into

sin with Bathsheba and God's never-ending promise to you in First John 1:9.)

3. In Proverbs 5:8 (*AMPC*), God gives us a powerful action step to escape the pitfalls of sexual sin. He says, "Let your way in life be far from her, and come not near the door of her house [avoid the very scenes of temptation]." Take time now to pray: *Lord, where am I repeatedly getting tripped up and falling into sin? What boundaries can I immediately put into place to avoid these scenes of temptation?*

LESSON 4

TOPIC

Idolatry, Witchcraft, Hatred, Variance

SCRIPTURES

1. **Galatians 5:16** — This I say then, Walk in the Spirit, and ye shall not fulfil the lust of the flesh.

2. **Galatians 5:19-21** — Now the works of the flesh are manifest, which are these; Adultery, fornication, uncleanness, lasciviousness, idolatry, witchcraft, hatred, variance, emulations, wrath, strife, seditions, heresies, envyings, murders, drunkenness, revellings, and such like....

3. **Acts 7:9** — And the patriarchs, [Joseph's brothers] moved with envy, sold Joseph into Egypt....

GREEK WORDS

1. "this I say" — Λέγω δέ (*Lego de*): I say categorically; I say emphatically

2. "walk" — περιπατέω (*peripateo*): a compound of the words περι (*peri*) and πατέω (*pateo*); the word περι (*peri*) means around and suggests the idea of something that is encircling; the word πατέω (*pateo*) means to walk and it denotes the movement of the feet; when compounded, to habitually walk around in one general vicinity; thus this word περιπατέω (*peripateo*) was often translated as the word 'live'

3. "shall not" — οὐ μὴ (*ou me*): the word οὐ (*ou*) is an emphatic no, with μὴ (*me*) which means no; you emphatically will not

4. "fulfil" — τελέω (*teleo*): to fulfill; to gratify; to satisfy

5. "lust" — ἐπιθυμία (*epithumia*): from ἐπί (*epi*) and θυμός (*thumos*); the word ἐπί (*epi*) means over and gives intensity to the word; the word θυμός (*thumos*) is passionate desire; when these words are compounded to form ἐπιθυμία (*epithumia*), it describes desire, cravings, or carnal longings of the flesh; one bent over and craving a thing

6. "flesh" — σαρκός (*sarkos*): flesh; carnal nature; base fleshly instincts

7. "works" —ἔργα (*erga*): labor or hard work

8. "manifest" — φανερός (*phaneros*): to appear, to manifest, to become visible, to become apparent, to become seen, to be well known, or to become conspicuous

9. "idolatry" — εἰδωλολατρεία (*eidololatreia*): a compound of the words εἴδωλον (*eidolon*) and λατρεία (*latreia*); the word εἴδωλον (*eidolon*) is Greek for a manmade idol, a heathen edifice, a pagan statue, or an image of a false god; the word λατρεία (*latreia*), derived from the word λατρεύω (*latreuo*), which means to work or to serve; it primarily has the meaning of one's extreme devotion and service to something he worships; in a positive sense, used in the Old Testament Greek Septuagint to depict the service of the priesthood who faithfully served and fulfilled their duties in the temple; but when λατρεύω (*latreuo*) is attached to the word εἴδωλον (*eidolon*), it forms the word εἰδωλολατρεία (*eidololatreia*), which depicts the worship of idols or idolatry

10. "witchcraft" — φαρμακεία (*pharmakeia*): the Greek word for medicines or drugs that inhibit a person's personality or change his behavior; mind-altering drugs; where we get the words pharmaceutical drugs or the word pharmacy; used in connection with sorcery, magic, or witchcraft

11. "hatred" — ἔχθρα (*echthra*): an intense hostility that one feels toward someone else; often used to picture enemies in a military conflict; in the New Testament, primarily denotes a personal enemy; depicts people who cannot get along with each other

12. "variance" — ἔρις (*eris*): used in a political context to describe political parties that had different platforms or agendas; some newer translations of the New Testament translates it as a party spirit

13. "emulations" — ζῆλος (*zelos*): in a negative sense, a person who is upset because someone else achieved more or received more; one who is jealous, envious, resentful, and filled with ill will for that other person who got what he wanted; as a result of not getting what he desired,

he is irritated, infuriated, irate, annoyed, provoked, and fuming that the
other person did get it; this person is incensed and ticked off

SYNOPSIS

The apostle Paul had a solid understanding of what happens when we live
to satisfy our fleshly, carnal nature. That's what prompted him to write this
candid warning to all believers in all generations: "Do not be deceived,
God is not mocked; for whatever a person sows, this he will also reap. For
the one who sows to his own flesh will reap destruction from the flesh,
but the one who sows to the Spirit will reap eternal life from the Spirit"
(Galatians 6:7,8 *NASB*).

Indeed, the works of the flesh only lead to heartache and misery. Thankfully we can escape this cycle of death and decay by learning to walk in the
Spirit. In this lesson, we will examine the next five works of the flesh listed
in Galatians 5:20: *idolatry, witchcraft, hatred, variance,* and *emulations.*

The emphasis of this lesson:

Idolatry **is when anything in your life takes first place above God.** *Witch-*
craft **is any do-it-yourself attempt to escape reality and not deal with the**
root of your problems. *Hatred* **is an intense hostility one feels toward**
another. *Variance* **is a 'party spirit' that divides and destroys relation-**
ships. And *emulations* **are basically envy and jealousy that move you to**
do hurtful things.

A REVIEW OF OUR ANCHOR VERSE

Galatians 5:16

To Walk in the Spirit
Means To *Live* in the Spirit

In Galatians 5:16, the apostle Paul gave this urgent charge: "This I say
then, Walk in the Spirit, and ye shall not fulfil the lust of the flesh"
(Galatians 5:16). His opening words, "This I say," are the Greek words
Lego de. The term *Lego* means *I say,* and the word *de* is very emphatic and
forceful. The use of these words signifies Paul raised his voice and said,
"Hey! I'm telling you emphatically and forcefully that if you walk in the
Spirit, you will not fulfill the lust of the flesh."

As we have seen in each previous lesson the word "walk" here is the Greek word *peripateo*, which is a compound of the words *peri* and *pateo*. The word *peri* means *around* and indicates something that is *encircling*, and the word *pateo* basically means *to walk down a path*. When these words are combined to form the word *peripateo*, it pictures *one who habitually walks around in one general vicinity all the time*. He or she walks and lives and spends their entire existence in one particular realm.

Therefore, "walking in the Spirit" could be translated as "living in the Spirit." It is a way of life, not a way we act just on Sundays. The path of the Spirit is meant to become our environment, our place of daily activity, and the sphere that encircles our existence. This should be the objective of every believer — including you.

Living in the Spirit Pulls the Plug on the Flesh

Paul said when you walk in the Spirit, "…Ye shall not fulfil the lust of the flesh" (Galatians 5:16). In Greek, the words "shall not" are the words *ou me*. The word *ou* means *emphatically no*, and the word *me* also means *no*. Together, they form a double negative that means *no, absolutely not, in no way*. Hence, when you habitually live in the Spirit, you cannot and will not in any way *fulfill* the lust of the flesh.

The word "fulfil" here is the Greek word *teleo*, and it means *to fulfill*; *to gratify*; or *to satisfy*. It depicts *something that starts out in an embryonic stage and grows up to reach full maturity*. What will not be fulfilled and "grow up and reach full maturity"? Paul said the "lust of the flesh." We've seen that the word "lust" here is the Greek word *epithumia*. It is a compound of the word *epi*, which means *over* and is an intensifier; and the word *thumos*, which describes *passionate desire*. When these words are joined to form *epithumia*, it depicts *desire, cravings, or carnal longings of the flesh*.

The word "flesh" is the Greek word *sarkos*, and it describes your *flesh*, *sinful impulses*, or *carnal instincts*. Thus, in the context of this verse, Paul is saying, "When you consistently live in the Spirit, you will put a stop to the development of the works of the flesh and sin in your life." Walking in the Spirit effectively pulls the plug on the works of the flesh.

Taking into account the original Greek meaning of the key words in this verse, here is the *Renner Interpretive Version (RIV)* of Galatians 5:16:

Make the path of the Spirit the place where you habitually live and walk. Become so comfortable on this spiritual path that you learn to leisurely and peacefully stroll along in that realm. Living your life in this Spirit realm is the best way to guarantee that you will not allow the yearnings of your flesh to creep out and fulfill themselves.

The Results of Walking in the Flesh Are Deadly

In Galatians 5:19, the apostle Paul went on to say, "Now the works of the flesh are manifest...." The word "works" here in Greek is the word *erga*, and it describes *labor* or *hard work*. It is some kind of *action*, *deed*, or *activity* that is generated by *one's labor* or by *one's effort or life*. What the flesh produces is *hard*, *painful work*. It is a life filled with excess, imbalance, laziness, self-abuse, hatred, strife, bitterness, irresponsibility, and neglect.

The way of the flesh is the hardest route for any individual to take. However, it is what we each naturally default to unless we take our flesh to the Cross and crucify it by the power of the Holy Spirit. Left unchecked, the flesh will keep screaming for us to surrender to it and allow it to manufacture its catastrophic consequences in our lives.

Paul wrote, "Now the works of the flesh are *manifest*..." (Galatians 5:19). In Greek, the word "manifest" is *phaneros*, and it means *to appear, to manifest, to become visible, to become apparent, to become seen, to be well known*, or *to become conspicuous*. Again, if you don't crucify your flesh — and keep it under control — the undesirable and damaging effects will become clearly visible to you and everyone else.

Galatians 5:19-21 lists 17 works of the flesh: "...Adultery, fornication, uncleanness, lasciviousness, idolatry, witchcraft, hatred, variance, emulations, wrath, strife, seditions, heresies, envyings, murders, drunkenness, revellings, and such like...." In our last lesson, we saw that adultery, fornication, uncleanness, and lasciviousness are all sexual sins. In this lesson, we will unearth the meaning of the next four works of the flesh, and they are: *idolatry, witchcraft, hatred, variance,* and *emulations*.

Idolatry Is When Anything in Your Life Takes First Place Above God

When most people hear the word "idolatry" they visualize a stone statue of a pagan god with wild, naked natives dancing in the light of a huge fire. But that's not what the apostle Paul had in mind when he included "idolatry" in the list of the works of the flesh.

The word "idolatry" is the Greek word *eidololatreia*. It is a compound of the words *eidolon* and *latreia*. The word *eidolon* is the Greek term for *a manmade idol, a heathen edifice, a pagan statue*, or *an image of a false god*. The word *latreia* is derived from the word *latreuo* — which means *to work* or *to serve*. It primarily has the meaning of *one's extreme devotion and service to something he worships*. In a positive sense, the word *latreia* was used in the Old Testament Greek Septuagint to depict the service of the priesthood who faithfully served and fulfilled their duties in the temple. However, when *latreuo* is attached to the word *eidolon*, it forms the word *eidololatreia*, which depicts *the worship of idols or idolatry*.

To be clear: Idolatry does not necessarily describe a physical idol. Idolatry transpires when a person gives his attention, devotion, passion, love, money, or commitment to a person, project, or object other than God. When something other than God takes first place in a person's mind, he has entered — at least to some measure — the sin of idolatry.

Idols were an offense to God in the Old Testament and they were forbidden to believers in the New Testament. God's hatred of idols is clearly demonstrated in First Samuel 5:1-4. Here we see the story of when the Philistines captured the Ark of the Covenant, which was a golden chest that held God's Presence. When the Philistines took it, they placed it on a ledge right next to an idol of their pagan god called "Dagon." When the Philistines came into their pagan temple the next morning, the Ark of the Covenant remained high on its ledge, but the statue of Dagon lay on the ground. Of course the Philistines wasted no time putting their idol back in its place. But the next morning they found Dagon lying on the ground again — this time facing downward, with its head and hands cut off!

God was making a statement. He refuses to share His space with any false god!

The fact is it's the nature of our flesh to become *obsessed*. If you're not careful, you can become obsessed with your family, your spouse, your parents, your children, your friends, your job, your dreams, your vision, your profession, your possessions, your school, your church activities, or even your own skills and talents. If any of these things intentionally or unintentionally becomes the focus of your worship and service, God will get involved to remove that object from your life.

You don't have to have a statue of a pagan god in your living room to be an idolater. If you are attempting to place any other person, project, or object in your life on the same level with God, you are committing a form of idolatry. If this is the case, it won't be long until God does something about it. As He shoved Dagon off its ledge and decapitated him in First Samuel 5:1-4, God will do something to get your attention! He will teach you that He is not willing to share His position of Lordship with anything or anyone else!

God isn't against you having any of the things mentioned above — family, spouse, parents, children, friends, a great job, dreams, vision, possessions, school, church activities, or personal talents — but God is against any of those things possessing you! Make sure that Jesus remains the primary focus of your life.

Witchcraft Is Any Attempt To Escape Reality And Not Deal With Root Issues

When most people hear the word *witchcraft*, they think of witches wearing all black, stirring a caldron, and riding on broomsticks. But that is not necessarily the case. In Galatians 5:20, the apostle Paul included this word as one of the works of the flesh. In Greek, the word for "witchcraft" is *pharmakeia* which is from where we get the words *pharmaceutical drugs* and *pharmacy*. It is the Greek term for *medicines or drugs that inhibit a person's personality or change his behavior. They are mind-altering drugs.* The word *pharmakeia* was used in New Testament times in connection with *sorcery, magic, or witchcraft.*

Why did Paul use the word "witchcraft" (*pharmakeia*) to depict one of the works of the flesh? When the Church of Jesus Christ was being established in the First Century, paganism ruled the Roman Empire. These were dark, demonic, pagan religions, and one prominent feature was the use of drugs to alter the state of one's mind.

When pagan worshipers were burdened and troubled by life, they came to pagan temples to find relief from their mental stresses, sicknesses, and a myriad of other personal problems. The pagan priests would take hallucinogenic drugs, pour them into vials of wine, stir it all together, and then give the mixture to worshipers to drink. Immediately, the drugs would take effect, and the pagan worshipers began to feel better.

After the recipients were medicated and under the influence of these mind-altering drugs, the priests would send them home and assure them that everything would be better. But once the drugs wore off, the worshipers found themselves facing the same or even worse problems. The only way these seekers found relief from their problems was to return to the pagan temples again and again for more drugs. Thus, these drugs gave people temporary relief but offered no permanent solution.

How does this apply to us today? Basically, in the context of Galatians 5:20, witchcraft is *any do-it-yourself attempt to escape reality and not deal with the root of our problems.* Although some people today do use mind-altering drugs and alcohol to feel better and forget about their problems, others escape reality by binge-watching movies and TV shows, partying with friends, buying things without restraint, or even sleeping excessively.

The flesh doesn't know how to fix itself or anyone else. In fact, the flesh doesn't even want to be fixed. Instead, it will try to convince a person to ignore his problem, to hide it with some superficial covering, or to drink alcohol or take drugs to make himself feel better. Yes, the alcohol and drugs may give that person a brief hiatus, but when the effects wear off, he will still have the same problems to deal with.

People who refuse to honestly look at themselves and find out what needs to change often develop chemical dependencies to cope with life or to avoid seeing the truth. You see, the flesh hates confrontation. Rather than look the facts squarely in the face, the flesh tries to run and hide, to sleep it off, or to preoccupy itself with recreational activities — anything to stay busy and keep from slowing down long enough to think about themselves and the issues they're facing. The flesh would rather try to learn how to cope then to be crucified and changed!

Now let's be clear. If your doctor has prescribed medication for you, by all means take your medication. What we are talking about here is spiritual advice, not medical advice. The point is, don't let your flesh tell you that you can keep covering up your problems with temporary solutions.

Eventually, temporary solutions will wear off or run out, and when they do, the same old you with the same old problems will resurface again.

Instead of trying more temporary solutions, let the Spirit of God deal with you and change you from the inside out forever! The Holy Spirit wants to identify the root of your problem and rip it out of your soul. He wants to bring permanent change to your life — if you will let Him.

Hatred Results From Long-Held Hurts and Offenses

The next work of the flesh Paul talks about is "hatred," which in Greek is the word *echthra*. This word describes *an intense hostility that one feels toward someone else* and was often used to picture *enemies in a military conflict*. In the New Testament, it primarily denotes *a personal enemy* or *people who cannot get along with each other*.

This word *echthra* is used in Luke 23:12 to depict the animosity, hostility, and hatred between Herod Antipas and Pilate before they became friends at the time of Jesus' trial and crucifixion. Prior to that moment, they hated each other. They were bitter, sour, hardened enemies who despised one another — and all of this is expressed in the Greek word *echthra*.

Basically, this word *echthra* — translated here as "hatred"— pictures people who cannot get along with each other. They have deep issues with each other — they hold resentments, grievances, complaints, and grudges that go way back in time and have very deep roots. Instead of letting go of the offense, they became divided, hostile, and fiercely opposed to each other. Now they are antagonistic, aggressive, and harsh. They hate each other and feel their hatred is justified.

Regardless of the severity of the offense we have endured, we cannot afford to hold on to unforgiveness toward an offender. Holding hatred in our hearts is deadly. God commands us to release and forgive those who mistreat us and even abuse us. No, we can't do this in our own strength. But we *can* do it in the power of the Holy Spirit. If you will pull the plug on the flesh and walk in the Spirit, it won't be long until that hostility and animosity is replaced with God's love, joy, peace, and longsuffering!

Variance Is a 'Party Spirit' That Divides and Destroys Relationships

In addition to idolatry, witchcraft, and hatred, the apostle Paul includes "variance" as a work of the flesh. The word for "variance" is the old Greek term *eris*, and it was used in a political context to describe *political parties that had different platforms or agendas.* Some newer translations of the New Testament translate this word as a *party spirit.*

In a democratic system, people align themselves politically with people of like opinions. Once they concur about their political views, they proceed to build a platform to promote their own agendas. Once the agenda is set, the competition begins and the fighting can be fierce. Undoubtedly, you have seen how deplorable political races can become. Nasty words are spoken, and lies are often told and repeated as facts. Moreover, false representations are publicized by opponents to discredit their contenders.

When Paul included the word "variance" in Galatians 5:20, he used the word *eris* to depict how flesh erupts to divide families, destroy relationships, ruin churches, and pull apart people who once stood side by side. Those who have been offended are drawn like a magnet to others who have been offended or who feel hurt. Once they discuss their feelings and realize they have similar stories or opinions, it isn't long before they start thinking they are right and everyone else is wrong!

They begin the process of building their own "platform" from which they begin to divide people and promote their own agenda! Thus, this word *eris* — "variance" — depicts a bitterly mean spirit that is so consumed with its own self-interests and self-ambitions that it would rather split and divide than to admit it is wrong or give an inch to an opponent!

This is exactly why churches split and families frequently dissolve. The flesh hates to surrender — or compromise — and admit it is wrong or let someone else be right. It would much rather blow issues out of proportion and wreak havoc than allow someone else have his way!

Emulations Are Essentially Envy and Jealousy

After Paul mentions variance, he includes another rather strange word — the word "emulations." In Greek, it is the word *zelos*, and in a negative sense, it depicts *a person who is upset because someone else achieved more or received more* than him. It is *one who is jealous, envious, resentful, and filled with ill will for that other person who got what he wanted.* As a result of not getting what he desired, he is irritated, infuriated, irate, annoyed, provoked, and fuming that the other person did get it. You might say this person is incensed and ticked off. He can't rejoice with the other person because he is so jealous.

A perfect example of the negative aspect of the word *zelos* is found in Acts 7:9 where it depicts the jealousy that Joseph's brothers felt for him. Here the Bible says, "And the patriarchs, [Joseph's brothers] moved with envy, sold Joseph into Egypt...." The words "moved with envy" are from the word *zelos*. This indicates that the brothers were incensed and ticked off at Joseph. After seeing him rewarded again and again by his father, they couldn't bear it any longer. Rather than rejoice that their younger brother was so loved, they cringed every time Joseph received a blessing. Eventually, they were filled with so much ill will toward Joseph and were so overcome by their jealousy that they sold him into slavery.

It's very important to note that Act 7:9 says they were "...moved with envy...." This word *zelos* — which essentially is *envy* or *jealousy* — is such a strong force that it will move you to action when it starts to operate in you. Unfortunately, it will move you to do things that are hurtful or that you will later regret.

So don't allow "emulations" (jealousy or envy) to work inside you! For that matter, don't allow idolatry, witchcraft, hatred, or variance to operate in you either. All these works of the flesh bring great hurt, pain, and destruction to you and others. Stop the madness before it starts. Learn to walk and live in the Spirit, and you will not satisfy and gratify the cravings of your flesh.

STUDY QUESTIONS

Study to shew thyself approved unto God, a workman that needeth not to be ashamed, rightly dividing the word of truth.
— 2 Timothy 2:15

1. After going through this thought-provoking lesson, what is your initial reaction? In what ways has your thinking, your attitudes, and your actions been challenged?

2. *Idolatry* does not necessarily describe a physical idol. Idolatry transpires when a person gives his or her attention, devotion, passion,
love, money, or commitment to a person, project, or object other than
God. Carefully meditate on the urgent warning in **First John 5:21**
(*AMPC*):

**"Little children, keep yourselves from idols (false gods) —
[from anything and everything that would occupy the place in
your heart due to God, from any sort of substitute for Him that
would take first place in your life]. Amen (so let it be)."**

Is there anything in your life that has become an idol to you? If so,
what is it? What do you sense the Holy Spirit is asking you to do to
give God first place again in your life?

3. *Hatred* is a work of the flesh describing people who can't get along
with each other. They're holding offenses, complaints, and grudges
that go way back in time. Does this describe you? What does Jesus
say about forgiving others in Matthew 6:14,15? If you're ready and
willing, God will give you the strength to *release, forgive*, and even *bless*
your offender (*see* 1 Peter 3:9). Simply pray and invite Him into your
situation and ask for His grace to do it (*see* James 4:6).

PRACTICAL APPLICATION

**But be ye doers of the word, and not hearers only,
deceiving your own selves.**
—James 1:22

1. The Bible says that "witchcraft" (*pharmakeia*) is a work of the flesh.
Essentially, it is any do-it-yourself attempt to escape reality and not
deal with the root of your problems. Be honest. Is there any area of
your life where this type of "witchcraft" is operating? If so, *where*?
What temporary solutions have you been relying on to self-medicate
the pain? Why not stop right now and surrender yourself to the One
who knows what's wrong and how to fix it?

2. In many ways, *variance* is closely related to hatred, except it results
in a distinct polarization of one person or group of people against
another. Have you ever experienced this in your church or family?
If so what caused the division? On what side did you find yourself?
What was the outcome of the situation?

3. Have you been — or are you — irritated, infuriated, annoyed, or fuming that someone else was blessed with something your heart had been longing for? It may be that your flesh is struggling with jealousy and envy (*emulations*). If so, pray and ask the Lord to show you the root cause of those intense feelings.

LESSON 5

TOPIC

Wrath, Strife, Seditions, Heresies

SCRIPTURES

1. **Galatians 5:16** — This I say then, Walk in the Spirit, and ye shall not fulfil the lust of the flesh.

2. **Galatians 5:19-21** — Now the works of the flesh are manifest, which are these; Adultery, fornication, uncleanness, lasciviousness, idolatry, witchcraft, hatred, variance, emulations, wrath, strife, seditions, heresies, envyings, murders, drunkenness, revellings, and such like....

GREEK WORDS

1. "this I say" — **Λέγω δέ** (*Lego de*): I say categorically; I say emphatically

2. "walk" — **περιπατέω** (*peripateo*): a compound of the words **περι** (*peri*) and **πατέω** (*pateo*); the word **περι** (*peri*) means around and suggests the idea of something that is encircling; the word **πατέω** (*pateo*) means to walk and it denotes the movement of the feet; when compounded, to habitually walk around in one general vicinity; thus this word **περιπατέω** (*peripateo*) was often translated as the word 'live'

3. "shall not" — **οὐ μὴ** (*ou me*): the word **οὐ** (*ou*) is an emphatic no, with **μὴ** (*me*) which means no; you emphatically will not

4. "lust" — **ἐπιθυμία** (*epithumia*): from **ἐπί** (*epi*) and **θυμός** (*thumos*); the word **ἐπί** (*epi*) means over and gives intensity to the word; the word **θυμός** (*thumos*) is passionate desire; when these words are compounded to form **ἐπιθυμία** (*epithumia*), it describes desire, cravings, or carnal longings of the flesh; one bent over and craving a thing

5. "flesh" — **σαρκός** (*sarkos*): flesh; carnal nature; base fleshly instincts

6. "works" — **ἔργα** (*erga*): labor or hard work

7. "wrath" — **θυμός** (*thumos*): used throughout the New Testament to picture one who is boiling with anger about something; although the person tries to restrain this anger by shoving it down deeper into his soul, it intermittently flares up; when it does, it is like a volcano that suddenly blows its top, scorching everything within its reach as it hurls its load of deadly molten lava onto the entire surrounding landscape; an outburst

8. "strife" — **ἐριθεία** (*eritheia*): a self-seeking ambition that is more concerned about itself and the fulfillment of its own wants, desires, and pleasures than it is in meeting the same needs in others; when *eritheia* is working in someone's life, it means that taking care of himself and getting what he wants is that person's principal concern; this is one so bent on getting what he wants that he is willing to do anything, say anything, and sacrifice any standard, rules, or relationship to achieve his goals; a selfish, self-focused attitude that is engrossed with its own desires and ambitions; so self-consumed that it is blinded to the desires or ambitions of other people

9. "seditions" — **διχοστασία** (*dichostasia*): a compound of the words **δίς** (*dis*) and **στάσις** (*stasis*); the word **δίς** (*dis*) means apart, as in a separation, and the word **στάσις** (*stasis*) means to stand; compounded, to stand apart, as one who rebels and steps away from someone to whom he should have been loyal; thus, the impression of disloyalty

10. "heresies" — **αἵρεσις** (*hairesis*): in the New Testament, a meaning that is unique and used differently than in secular literature; the idea of a person or group of people who are sectarian; the word "sectarian" refers to adherents of a sect that is usually limited in scope and closed to outsiders, staying primarily to themselves; in New Testament times, such groups were considered to be unauthorized because they were not submitted to the authority of the church leadership

SYNOPSIS

Jesus made a compelling statement concerning the power of the Holy Spirit and the significance of the flesh. He said, "It is the Spirit Who gives life [He is the Life-giver]; the flesh conveys no benefit whatever [there is no profit in it]…" (John 6:63 *AMPC*). What a sobering declaration from the lips of Jesus! There is absolutely *no profit* or *benefit* from the flesh.

Indeed, the only thing we can count on from the work of the flesh is *hard*, *problematic* consequences. The flesh has a mind of its own — a mind that is poisoned by sin and totally opposed to the things of God. As we have seen in the last few lessons, the works of the flesh includes things like adultery, fornication, uncleanness, lasciviousness, idolatry, witchcraft, hatred, variance, and emulations (*see* Galatians 5:19,20). In this lesson, we will examine four more works of the flesh: *wrath*, *strife*, *seditions*, and *heresies*.

The emphasis of this lesson:

Wrath is unresolved anger boiling within a person that inevitably explodes onto others. *Strife* is selfish ambition that is more focused on its own wants and needs than anyone else's. *Seditions* are disloyalty and rebellion to established authority. And *heresies* are unauthorized groups formed out of divisiveness.

A REVIEW OF OUR ANCHOR VERSE

Galatians 5:16

'Walk in the Spirit'

In Galatians 5:16, the apostle Paul gave the Church of the Lord Jesus Christ this urgent directive: "This I say then, Walk in the Spirit, and ye shall not fulfil the lust of the flesh." When Paul says, "This I say," he employed the Greek words *Lego de*. The word *Lego* means *I say*, and the word *de* describes something *emphatic* and *categorical*. It is the equivalent of Paul raising his voice and speaking in the strongest language saying, "Hey, I'm telling you emphatically and categorically that if you walk in the Spirit, you will not fulfill the lust of the flesh."

We have seen that the word "walk" here is the Greek word *peripateo*, which is a compound of the words *peri* and *pateo*. The word *peri* means *around* and indicates something that is *encircling*, and the word *pateo* is a Greek word that means *to walk*. When these words come together and form the word *peripateo*, it means *to habitually walk around in one general vicinity all the time*. It is the picture of someone who has walked and walked on a certain path for so long it has become their way of life.

Thus, "walking in the Spirit" actually means "living in the Spirit." The original Greek here depicts a person who has walked in one area for such a long time it has now become his environment and the realm that encircles his existence.

It's God's Guarantee
How Not To Fulfill the Lust of the Flesh

The Bible says when you walk in the Spirit, "...Ye shall not fulfil the lust of the flesh" (Galatians 5:16). We've learned that the words "shall not" are the Greek words *ou me*. The word *ou* means *emphatically no*, and the word *me* also means *no*. When *ou* and *me* are compounded, it becomes a double negative that means *no, you emphatically will not*. This means when you walk in the Spirit, *you emphatically will not, no not ever,* fulfill the lust of the flesh.

The word "fulfil" here is the Greek word *teleo*, which means *to fulfill; to gratify;* or *to satisfy*. And the word "lust" is the Greek word *epithumia*. It is a compound of the word *epi*, which means *over* and gives intensity to the word; and the word *thumos*, which describes *passionate desire*. When these words come together to form *epithumia*, it depicts *desire, cravings, or carnal longings of the flesh*. Because the intensifying word *epi* is included, it is a picture of the flesh doubled over, yearning and craving for something.

Paul specifies that the lust is of the "flesh." In Greek, "flesh" is the word *sarkos*, and it describes *the flesh; carnal cravings;* or *sinful impulses*. The only way to effectively deal with your flesh is to crucify it. If you don't crucify it and keep it under control, it will manifest its evil fruits. That is, the flesh will go to work and begin producing all kinds of deadly results.

Taking into account the original Greek meaning of the key words in this verse, here is the *Renner Interpretive Version (RIV)* of Galatians 5:16:

Make the path of the Spirit the place where you habitually live and walk. Become so comfortable on this spiritual path that you learn to leisurely and peacefully stroll along in that realm. Living your life in this Spirit realm is the best way to guarantee that you will not allow the yearnings of your flesh to creep out and fulfill themselves.

The 'Works' of the Flesh Will 'Manifest'

In Galatians 5:19, the apostle Paul continued by saying, "Now the *works* of the flesh are manifest…." In Greek, the word "works" is the word *erga*, which describes *labor* or *hard work*. It implies some kind of *action, deed*, or *activity* and often refers to *the things produced by someone's effort or life*. What the flesh produces is *hard, laborious work*. Indeed, a life dominated by the flesh is a *hard life*.

Again, the Bible says, "Now the works of the flesh are *manifest…*" (Galatians 5:19). This word "manifest" is the Greek word *phaneros*, and it means *to appear, to manifest, to become visible, to become apparent, to become seen, to be well known,* or *to become conspicuous*. Essentially, what this is telling us is that all the nasty and obnoxious characteristics that are hiding in your flesh will be brought out into the open for all to see unless you crucify your flesh — and keep it under control.

Here are the works of the flesh included in Galatians 5:19-21: "…Adultery, fornication, uncleanness, lasciviousness, idolatry, witchcraft, hatred, variance, emulations, wrath, strife, seditions, heresies, envyings, murders, drunkenness, revellings, and such like…." We learned that the first four works — adultery, fornication, uncleanness, and lasciviousness — are all sexual sins. The four works of the flesh we are going to examine now are all matters that will adversely affect your relationships.

Wrath Is Unresolved Anger Boiling Within That Will Inevitably Explode

Paul includes "wrath" as one of the works of the flesh, and it is the Greek word *thumos*, which is used throughout the New Testament to picture *one who is boiling with anger about something*. Although this person tries to restrain his anger by shoving it down deeper into his soul, it intermittently flares up. When it does, it is like a volcano that suddenly blows its top — scorching everything within its path as it hurls its load of deadly molten lava onto the entire surrounding landscape.

Have you ever seen someone blow his top like this? That is what the Greek word *thumos*, translated "wrath," vividly depicts. How does wrath develop in a person? Usually it happens when people get hurt, offended, or upset, and rather than take the offense to the Cross and deal with it there, they choose to shove the memory deeper into their soul — all the while meditating on the perceived offense over and over again. The longer they think about it, the more upset they become.

Soon they are inwardly boiling about what took place. They know if they don't do something quickly to restrain themselves, they are going to say or do something really ugly. Therefore, they once again try to shove it back down deep inside in an attempt to keep it under control. But if those angry emotions are never properly dealt with by the Holy Spirit, eventually something will happen that triggers their release.

Perhaps this has happened to you. If so, you may think those vile emotions are gone. But if you never let the Lord really deal with them — or the situation that created them — they're still lying dormant inside you just waiting for the moment to be released again.

How might they be released? It may be that you are with the same person who made you angry in the first place — or in a similar situation. As the familiar, undesirable scenario begins to play out once again, those raw feelings of anger and bitterness that were boiling inside will suddenly begin to erupt in harsh and explosive words. It's almost as if someone opens a door on the inside of you, releasing a flood of red-hot, rank emotions that come spewing out of your mouth! At that point, you can become unglued — saying things you later regret and speaking in tones you should never use!

That is what "wrath" — the Greek word *thumos* — looks like. It is the way the flesh tries to deal with problems. Rather than confront the issue head-on when it happens, the flesh says, "Just shove it down deep, and keep it to yourself!" The problem is, when you try to bury unresolved issues deep in your soul, they just keep churning and boiling, awaiting the next opportunity to erupt.

Even though the flesh is attempting to avoid confrontation, in the end its eruption creates a confrontation more scorching and hurtful than ever. It would have been far better to deal with the issue when it first happened!

Strife Is Essentially Selfish Ambition

Next on the list of works of the flesh is "strife." In Greek, this is the word *eritheia*, and it describes *a self-seeking ambition that is more concerned about itself and the fulfillment of its own wants, desires, and pleasures than it is in meeting the same needs in others.* When this kind of "strife" — the Greek word *eritheia* — is working in someone's life, it means that taking care of himself and getting what he wants is this person's principal concern.

A strife-filled person is one so bent on getting what he wants that he is willing to do anything, say anything, and sacrifice any standard, rule, or relationship to achieve his goals. Thus, "strife" (*eritheia*) is *a selfish, self-focused attitude that is engrossed with its own desires and ambitions.* In fact, it is so self-consumed that it is blinded to the desires or ambitions of other people. When someone has this attitude, he is bound to hurt and to offend others.

Maybe you know someone like this. As you read through the description, you possibly could see their face in your mind. It is a person so committed to his own cause that he can't see anything but himself. If someone mentions something other than his own cause or projects, he immediately turns the conversation back to him because he can't tolerate anyone talking about anything or anyone else. This characteristic of his gives the impression of conceit and extreme selfishness.

Friend, don't let this be you! If you hear yourself talking nonstop about your own projects, dreams, and aspirations — but you never stop to inquire about anyone else's — this work of the flesh may very well be operating in you. If so, let God speak to you about selfishness in your life.

From time to time, you will have to deliberately speak to the carnal nature and tell it to be quiet so you can recognize and meet the needs of those around you. God's Spirit is inside you, and if you will yield to the Holy Spirit, He will make you compassionate, caring, and aware of the needs of others.

Seditions Are Disloyalty and Rebellion to Authority

In addition to wrath and strife, the apostle Paul said "seditions" is also a work of the flesh. In Greek, the word "seditions" is *dichostasia*, which is a compound of the words *dis* and *stasis*. The word *dis* means *apart*, as in a *separation*; and the word *stasis* means *to stand*. When these words are compounded, it means *to stand apart, as one who rebels and steps away from someone to whom he should have been loyal.* Thus, "seditions" is essentially disloyalty.

This very word — *dichostasia* — is used in Matthew, Mark, and Luke to describe the insurrection that Barabbas had led in the city of Jerusalem.

His rebellious deeds deemed him a notorious criminal to Roman authorities. He had led an insurrection, a *sedition* — an act of *dichostasia*. Barabbas defied the governing powers, rejected their authority, and stepped away from their rule — taking other rebels with him as he went his own way. As often happens when seditious flesh has its way, Barabbas united all the rebels in the city together in an attempt to overthrow the government.

When a person gets involved in *seditions*, he never rebels alone. He always takes people with him, usually gathering a crowd of others who are just as offended if not more offended with the same established authority. Once a group is formed, they all walk away from authority together. *Sedition* — the act of *dichostasia* — was the ultimate act of defiance or disloyalty to an established authority.

It is important for you to know that the flesh hates rules, regulations, and any order imposed upon it. This is why children rebel against parents, church congregations rebel against pastors, and people in general rebel against God. The flesh simply doesn't want to be told what to do!

This is even the reason a beautiful little baby throws his food across the room! When a baby acts like that, it makes one wonder how in the world such an innocent-looking child could behave so badly. But the reason a young child can act so defiantly is that he is wrapped in flesh — and one of the works of the flesh is to be rebellious and defiant!

Defiance and rebellion to authority is the source of most wars. Ninety-nine percent of the world's conflicts are due to flesh that refuses to be told what to do and then rises up to defy the authority or the rules it doesn't want to accept!

So when you find your flesh rising up in anger because your boss, your parent, or your pastor acts like he or she has authority in your life, it's time for you to settle down and mortify the deeds of your flesh! Don't give in to your carnal desires by stepping away from your God-appointed leader. If you do, you may find yourself in a company of rebels like Barabbas.

Please know that your disloyalty is hurtful and destructive. So remain loyal and stick close to those whom God has called to be your leaders — and be faithful!

Heresies Are Unauthorized Groups
That Form Out of Divisiveness

Paul closes out Galatians 5:20 listing "heresies" as yet another work of the flesh. In Greek, the word "heresies" is *hairesis*, and in the New Testament, this word has a unique meaning that is very different than how it was used in secular literature of the First Century. It carries the idea of a person or group of people who are *sectarian*, which refers to adherents of a *sect* that is usually limited in scope and closed to outsiders, staying primarily to themselves. In Early New Testament times, such groups were considered to be unauthorized because they were not submitted to the authority of the church leadership.

In today's contemporary language, we would label these sectarian groups as "cliques." Again, these are groups of people who believe or conduct themselves as if they are *exclusive*. They give the impression that they are better or more enlightened than those outside the group — or that they have a special assignment that no one else can know about. This is the reason they keep outsiders on the outside and allow so few to have an inside peek at their fellowship, meetings, conversations, or activities.

The word "heresies" (*hairesis*) primarily suggests *a division, a faction*, or as noted, *an unauthorized group*. Because this kind of group was viewed to be so disruptive to the Early Church — and because it didn't fall under the spiritual covering of church leadership — the apostle Paul viewed it to be heretical, which means very *divisive*. He was against such spiritual elitism and even forbade it! This is likely why he included it in his list of the works of the flesh in Galatians 5:19-21.

The adherents to such heresies usually followed a leader who was not the pastor but who acted as if he had spiritual authority — even though authority had never been given to him by the church leadership. This leader usually demanded the highest commitment from group members — even demanding his followers' commitment to himself and to the group be greater than their commitment to the overall church body.

Let's face it — the flesh delights in deceiving itself into believing that it's better, more spiritual, or more enlightened than anyone else. It thrives on being puffed up, prideful, and boastful. It enjoys thinking too highly of itself, and if allowed to do so, the flesh will separate into a faction — a heresy, a division, or a sect. It will gravitate to others whose flesh also wants to believe they are better than others. When all that flesh gets together in one place, they will inevitably form a super-elite clique that is so tight no one else will be able to get in it.

Never lose sight of the fact that you are a part of the whole Body of Christ. God has not given you or anyone else a revelation or truth so special that it is only for a handful. So don't let your flesh deceive you into thinking you are a member of a higher spiritual class! Tell your flesh to come back down to reality and get busy loving and serving others in the local church!

Friend, God has made a way for you to escape fulfilling the lusts of the flesh, and it is by walking in the Spirit! Once more, here is the *Renner Interpretive Version (RIV)* of Galatians 5:16:

> **Make the path of the Spirit the place where you habitually live and walk. Become so comfortable on this spiritual path that you learn to leisurely and peacefully stroll along in that realm. Living your life in this Spirit realm is the best way to guarantee that you will not allow the yearnings of your flesh to creep out and fulfill themselves.**

In our next lesson, we will carefully look at the final four works of the flesh listed in Galatians 5:21, which are *envyings, murders, drunkenness,* and *revellings.*

STUDY QUESTIONS

> **Study to shew thyself approved unto God, a workman that needeth not to be ashamed, rightly dividing the word of truth.**
> **— 2 Timothy 2:15**

1. God wants each of us to have a healthy, humble view of ourselves, which is why He included verses in the Bible like Romans 12:3 and Philippians 2:3,4. Take time to look up these two scriptures in a few different Bible translations and write out the version that speaks to you most deeply.

2. The Bible says that as believers, we are all members of the *Body of Christ.* To keep us from getting puffed up in pride, the Holy Spirit prompted Paul to write First Corinthians 12:12-27. Take a few moments to reflect on this passage. How do Paul's words encourage

you to know you have value? How do they help you appreciate the gifts in others? What else is the Holy Spirit speaking to you through this passage?

3. *Seditions* and *heresies* are two works of the flesh that deal with not wanting to yield to authority. What does God say about all authority in Romans 13:1-7 — especially in verse 1 and 2? How does this passage challenge your attitudes, actions, and thinking toward those in authority?

PRACTICAL APPLICATION

But be ye doers of the word, and not hearers only,
deceiving your own selves.
—James 1:22

1. Have you ever felt like a ticking time bomb waiting to explode? Does it seem as though feelings of anger and bitterness are often boiling just below the surface? If so, you're likely dealing with wrath. Take a few moments and pray: *Lord, why am I so angry? Who has hurt or offended me? Please show me so that I can surrender this person (or people) and the situation (or situations) to You and repent and receive the forgiveness and healing I need.*

2. Are you mindful of others? Do the people in your life know all about you but you know nothing about them? Do you think about ways you can be a blessing to them, or do you always think of how others can be a blessing to you? If your answer is yes, what does this tell you about your attitude toward other people?

3. Do you know anyone who has acted *seditiously* — rejecting the established authority of the government, local law enforcement, or even the Church? What were they so up in arms about? Did they draw others to their rebellious cause? What was the outcome of their choices and behavior?

TOPIC

Envyings, Murders, Drunkenness, Revellings

SCRIPTURES

1. **Galatians 5:16** — This I say then, Walk in the Spirit, and ye shall not fulfil the lust of the flesh.

2. **Galatians 5:19-21** — Now the works of the flesh are manifest, which are these; Adultery, fornication, uncleanness, lasciviousness, idolatry, witchcraft, hatred, variance, emulations, wrath, strife, seditions, heresies, envyings, murders, drunkenness, revellings, and such like....

3. **Mark 15:10** — For he knew that the chief priests had delivered him for envy.

4. **Ephesians 5:18** — And be not drunk with wine, wherein is excess....

5. **2 Timothy 3:4** — Traitors, heady, highminded, lovers of pleasures more than lovers of God.

GREEK WORDS

1. "this I say" — **Λέγω δέ** (*Lego de*): I say categorically; I say emphatically

2. "walk" — **περιπατέω** (*peripateo*): a compound of the words **περι** (*peri*) and **πατέω** (*pateo*); the word **περι** (*peri*) means around and suggests the idea of something that is encircling; the word **πατέω** (*pateo*) means to walk and it denotes the movement of the feet; when compounded, to habitually walk around in one general vicinity; thus this word **περιπατέω** (*peripateo*) was often translated as the word 'live'

3. "shall not" — **οὐ μὴ** (*ou me*): the word **οὐ** (*ou*) is an emphatic no, with **μὴ** (*me*) which means no; you emphatically will not

4. "lust" — **ἐπιθυμία** (*epithumia*): from **ἐπί** (*epi*) and **θυμός** (*thumos*); the word **ἐπί** (*epi*) means over and gives intensity to the word; the word **θυμός** (*thumos*) is passionate desire; when these words are compounded to form **ἐπιθυμία** (*epithumia*), it describes desire, cravings, or carnal longings of the flesh; one bent over and craving a thing

5. "flesh" — **σαρκός** (*sarkos*): flesh; carnal nature; base fleshly instincts

6. "works" — **ἔργα** (*erga*): labor or hard work

7. "envyings" — **φθόνος** (*phthonos*): a hostile feeling toward someone because he has something, such as an advantage, a benefit, or a position, that the other does not possess but would like to have; a despicable feeling toward a person with a perceived advantage that is so strong the one who feels "envy" takes action to remove that person's advantage in the hope that it will pass on to him; a kind of envy that is evil, sinister, and full of maliciousness

8. "drunkenness" — **μέθη** (*methe*): strong drink or drunkenness; the consumption of wine for the sake of intoxication

9. "excess" — **ἀσωτία** (*asotia*): one who has lost his ability to save or to spare himself; a loss of control

10. "revellings" — **κῶμος** (*komos*): here plural, a festive procession or merrymaking

11. "lovers of pleasures" — **φιλήδονος** (*philedonos*): a compound of the words **φίλος** (*philos*) and **ἡδονή** (*hedone*); the word **φίλος** (*philos*) means to love, and the word **ἡδονή** (*hedone*) means something that tastes sweet or something that is pleasant or enjoyable; of the five times where the word *hedone* is used in the New Testament, it is used in a bad sense to describe the unrestrained seeking of carnal pleasures

SYNOPSIS

If you've ever wondered how destructive following your flesh can be, listen to these sobering words from the apostle Paul: "Now the mind of the flesh [which is sense and reason *without* the Holy Spirit] is death [death that comprises all the miseries arising from sin, both here and hereafter]. But the mind of the [Holy] Spirit is life and [soul] peace [both now and forever]" (Romans 8:6 *AMPC*).

Wow! Is it any wonder Paul urged us to walk in the Spirit? Is it any surprise he said, "…Set your minds and keep them set on what is above (the higher things), not on the things that are on the earth" (Colossians 3:2 *AMPC*). If you want to escape the problems that come with living a life dominated by the flesh, then throw your arms wide open to living a life led by the Spirit. As you do, the peace of God will saturate your soul!

The emphasis of this lesson:

Envyings are hostile, malicious feelings toward others who appear to have something we're longing for. When envy is allowed to fester, *murders* are the result. *Drunkenness* is the consumption of alcohol for the sake of intoxication; it always leads to unrestrained, fleshly expression. And a person who constantly seeks to be entertained is ensnared by *revellings*.

A QUICK REVIEW OF OUR ANCHOR VERSE
Galatians 5:16

In Galatians 5:16, the apostle Paul said, "This I say then, Walk in the Spirit, and ye shall not fulfill the lust of the flesh." As we have seen in previous lessons, the words **"this I say"** in Greek is *Lego de*. The word *Lego* means *I say*, and it is a very strong declaration by itself. To this Paul added the word *de*, which describes something that is *absolute, categorical*, or *emphatic*.

Here we see a picture of Paul lifting his voice loudly and firmly saying. "Hear me! I'm going to tell you something *absolutely true, emphatic*, and *categorical. If you walk in the Spirit you shall not fulfill the lust of the flesh.*"

We have determined that this word "walk" doesn't describe a hit or miss visit or a once-a-week Sunday stopover when you're in a good mood. This word **"walk"** is the Greek word *peripateo*, which is a compound of the words *peri* and *pateo*. The word *peri* means *around* and signifies something that is *encircling*. And the word *pateo* is the Greek word that means *to walk*. When these words are compounded to form the word *peripateo*, it depicts *one who habitually walks around in one general vicinity all the time*. It is the picture of someone who has walked and walked on a certain path for so long it has become their place of existence.

This lets us know that one who *walks* in the Spirit is one who lives in the Spirit; it is where he conducts his entire life. That is what this word *peripateo* means. Paul is telling us that we can actually *live* in the Spirit. It is something we can do through Christ who gives us strength (*see* Philippians 4:13). And when we live in the Spirit, we shall not fulfill the lust of the flesh.

We've pointed out in our previous lessons that the words **"shall not"** in Greek are *ou me*. The word *ou* is emphatic for *no*, and the Greek word *me* also means *no*. When we put these words together, it forms a double negative that literally means, *"Emphatically no, in no way will you fulfill the lust of the flesh."* This tells us that when we operate in the realm of the Spirit, we won't function out of the realm of the flesh.

This brings us to the word **"lust,"** the Greek word *epithumia*. It is a compound of the words *epi* and *thumos*. The word *epi* means *over*, and the word *thumos* describes *passionate desire*. When these words are compounded to form *epithumia*, it describes *desire, cravings, or carnal longings of the flesh*. It pictures someone yearning and craving something so desperately he is doubled over longing for it.

Paul says these carnal cravings and longings are of the "flesh," which is the Greek word *sarkos*, and it describes *the flesh*; *carnal nature*; or *base fleshly instincts*. Make no mistake: Your flesh has a mind and will of its own, and if you don't put it to death by the power of the Holy Spirit, it will bring destruction and devastation into your life. However, if you choose to live in the Spirit, you will effectively pull the plug on the flesh.

Taking into account the original Greek meaning of the key words in this verse, here is the *Renner Interpretive Version (RIV)* of Galatians 5:16:

> **Make the path of the Spirit the place where you habitually live and walk. Become so comfortable on this spiritual path that you learn to leisurely and peacefully stroll along in that realm. Living your life in this Spirit realm is the best way to guarantee that you will not allow the yearnings of your flesh to creep out and fulfill themselves.**

In Galatians 5:19, the apostle Paul went on to write, "Now the works of the flesh are manifest...." The word "works" here is the Greek word *erga*, which describes *labor* or *hard work*. Clearly, what the flesh produces is *problematic* and *grueling*, and left undealt with, the flesh — your carnal nature — will "manifest" its works. That is, the results of your fleshly instincts running your life will become *visibly evident* to you and everyone else.

The Bible itemizes 17 works of the flesh in Galatians 5:19-21, and they are: "...Adultery, fornication, uncleanness, lasciviousness, idolatry, witchcraft, hatred, variance, emulations, wrath, strife, seditions, heresies, envyings, murders, drunkenness, revellings, and such like...." For the remainder of this lesson, we will focus on the meanings of *envyings*, *murders*, *drunkenness*, and *revellings*.

Envyings Are Hostile, Malicious Feelings Toward Others

The word "envyings" in Galatians 5:21 is the Greek word *phthonos*, and it describes *a hostile feeling toward someone because he has something — an advantage, a benefit, a position — that the other does not possess but would like to have.* This is a despicable feeling toward a person with a perceived advantage. This feeling is so strong that the one who feels "envy" takes action to remove that person's advantage in the hope that it will pass on to him. This word "envyings"(*phthonos*) depicts a kind of envy that is evil, sinister, and full of maliciousness.

An example of this intense type of envy is found in Mark 15:10, when the Jewish leaders turned Jesus over to Pilate to be criminally tried in a court of law. Scripture says, "For he knew that the chief priests had delivered him [Jesus] for envy." Pilate could see the real motives of the chief priests and knew why they arrested Jesus.

The chief priests felt threatened and insecure because of Jesus' surging popularity in the nation. Pilate knew that insecurity was the driving motivation of the chief priests to demand that Jesus be charged with a criminal offense and be crucified. They wanted to remove Jesus so the publicity He was receiving would be shifted back to them — where it had been before Jesus came on the scene.

This Greek word *phthonos* — translated here as "envying" — implies *a deeply felt grudge because one possesses what a person wishes was his own.* Because the person has envy, he begrudges what that other person possesses and is covetous of that person's belongings, accomplishments, relationships, or titles in life. Every time he sees that other person, he inwardly seethes about his success. He deeply resents that other person's blessing and tries to figure out a way to seize it away from the person to make it his own.

In the above example, the chief priests were envious of the popularity of Jesus. To get rid of the competition, they decided to kill Jesus. That's the way this type of envy reacts. It is so strong that it propels a person to take some kind of action — most often some kind of evil action designed to do away with the person who has the advantage.

Murders Are the Result of Unbridled Envy

It's interesting to note that in the original Greek text of Galatians 5:21, the word "murders" does not appear. It seems very likely that the intensity of the word "envyings" explains why the *King James Version* adds the word "murders." The translators perceived this "envy" to be so strong that it would even drive a person to "murder" in order to get what he wants.

There are also examples in literature where the word *phthonos* (envyings) is also used to represent a person who uses others as a steppingstone to get where he or she wants to be in terms of money, prestige, and power. This is an unscrupulous person who uses people to get what he wants.

Perhaps you've seen this work of the flesh at your place of employment — or maybe even at church. When a fellow employee — or believer — tried to snuggle up close to you and be your best friend, but you found out later that the person was only pretending to be your friend. In reality, he didn't want to be your friend. He just wanted to get close to you so he could befriend someone you knew. In order to connect with that other person, he had to go through you. So he acted like your friend in order to gain the advantage and then dropped you like a lead balloon.

Perhaps someone said they wanted to be your friend — but he really wanted your job! This goes on in the secular world all the time, but it should not happen in the Church. Such behavior is hurtful, manipulative, and unkind. It wounds souls, cheapens the concept of friendship, and makes people feel like they have been abused. No wonder Paul calls "envy" a work of the flesh!

The next time you find yourself tempted to get envious over someone else's blessing or position, call on the Spirit of God to help you mortify that deed of the flesh. Shut it down and shut it up by deliberately choosing to rejoice when someone else gets blessed! What you sow is exactly what you will reap. If you sow anger, resentment, and bitterness, that is the harvest that will come back to you. But if — by the power of the Holy Spirit — you sow sincere rejoicing and celebration, that's what you'll receive.

Drunkenness Is Intoxication
That Leads to Unrestrained Fleshly Expression

Next on the list of works of the flesh is "drunkenness," which is a translation of the Greek word *methe*. It describes *strong drink* or *drunkenness* or *the consumption of wine for the sake of intoxication*. This was common in the First Century due to many pagan religions that used wine as a part of their religious practices.

For example, take the religion of Bacchus, which was also known as Dionysos. It was centered around wine and intoxication. In fact, Bacchus (or Dionysos) was called the god of wine. Once the worshipers were completely inebriated from their consumption of wine, they threw off all restraints and yielded themselves to the flesh. Nothing was off limits. Consequently, they would plunge themselves into the most vulgar sexual excesses and unnatural acts. The participants breached every known moral code and committed the grossest sin possible.

While under the influence of wine, people fornicated while pagan priests beat drums and clanged cymbals to add to the rage and passion of the moment. Often drugs were mixed together with the wine, which caused the participants to convulse or dance in frenzied circles. This frenzied condition was called *entheos* — a compound of the words *en* and *theos*. The word *en* means *in*, and *theos* is the word for *god*. Thus, if a person was *entheos*, he was said to be "in the control of a god." Interestingly, this is where we get the word *enthusiasm*. When a participant fell into one of these frenzied moments, he passed the barrier and was caught in the control of a god or spirit. This *entheos* experience was the ultimate goal for those who participated.

The use of wine was a widespread practice in nearly all pagan religions. Archaeological digs testify to the prevalent use of wine at that time. A large number of homes excavated reveal the presence of underground tanks to hold a large supply of wine. When residents had finished the wine they had on hand, they would simply lower a bucket down into their storage tank and pull it up so they could keep drinking.

The fact that there was this much wine available in homes demonstrates the central role wine played in First-Century society. Paul knew that when flesh became absorbed with wine, a person lost his ability to think rationally, and it often led to devastating excess. This is why he told the

Ephesian believers, "And be not drunk with wine, wherein is excess..."
(Ephesians 5:18). The word "excess" here is *asotia*, and it depicts *one who has lost his ability to save or to spare himself* or *a loss of control*.

When a person's mind has been altered by excessive alcohol, he or she thinks irrationally, acts irresponsibly, and commits acts of *excess* that normally would not be a temptation. Under the influence of alcohol, he wastes his life, squanders his money, and desecrates his body because he is drunk and he cannot think straight. In that drunken state, his ability to think correctly has been suppressed, and his flesh has been released to wrongfully express itself.

The believers in the First Century were trying to walk free from the power of their flesh. The last thing they needed was to drink wine and inhibit their ability to think correctly. Excessive alcohol consumption only serves to revive the flesh and cause people to do things that are sinful and damaging!

That is why Paul urged them to leave the wine alone! Its consumption only leads to the works of the flesh. Instead, Paul urged them to "be filled with the Spirit." Being filled and staying filled with the Holy Spirit has a spiritually intoxicating effect that produces wonderful results!

A Person Who Constantly Seeks To Be Entertained Is Ensnared by *Revellings*

The last work of the flesh listed by the apostle Paul in Galatians 5:21 is "revellings," which is the Greek word *komos*. Here it is plural, and it describes *a festive procession* or *constant merrymaking*. When most people hear the word "revellings," they imagine it refers to drunkenness, street fights, or people who run from one drunken party to the next. But that is not the case.

"Revellings" — the Greek word *komos* — actually describes *a person who can't bear the thought of boredom and continually seeks for different forms of amusement or entertainment*. This person is so afraid of being bored that he or she constantly contemplates what they can do next to be entertained. This word can also refer to a person who endlessly eats at parties or who seeks constant laughter.

Now, there is nothing wrong with laughter. The problem is this person is *consumed* with the need for comedy, light moments, fun, pleasure, entertainment, or constant eating. He lives for the next meal, the next restaurant, the next movie, or the next vacation.

In Second Timothy 3:4, the Holy Spirit prophesied through Paul that this kind of hedonism would be prevalent in the last days. He said people would be, "traitors, heady, highminded, *lovers of pleasures* more than lovers of God." The phrase "lovers of pleasures" is a translation of the Greek word *philedonos*, a compound of the words *philos* and *hedone*. The word *philos* means *to love*, and the word *hedone* describes *something that tastes sweet* or *something that is pleasant or enjoyable*. Of the five times where the word *hedone* is used in the New Testament, it is used in a bad sense to describe *the unrestrained seeking of carnal pleasures*. By using the word *philedonos*, translated "lovers of pleasures," Paul explicitly said that in the last days, people will be obsessed with pleasure.

Do you see why Paul included "revellings" in his list of the works of the flesh in Galatians 5:19-21? Revellings is the flesh's ongoing attempt to escape responsibility and avoid the seriousness of life. If you let your flesh lead you, it will waste your time, your talent, and your energy. You'll end up spending the majority of your days watching television, going to movies, eating at restaurants, and in the end, you'll have nothing to show for it but tons of credit card debt.

The flesh says, "Come on, it will feel so good if you do this. It's true that you probably shouldn't, but just one more time won't hurt. Besides, what else do you have to do? There's nothing to do at home!" The truth is there's plenty to do at home! You could be reading your Bible and praying, developing your relationship with your spouse, playing with your children, spending time with your brothers and sisters, visiting neighbors, taking care of your yard, cleaning your garage, serving in some area of your church, learning to cook, or reading a book and developing your mind. The truth is, there is a host of things you could do that would be healthy for you and your family!

So the next time your flesh says "There's nothing to do! It's so boring!" Evaluate the health of your relationships… Take a look inside your garage… Check the condition of your backyard… Peek into your clothes closet. I think you'll see that there is plenty for you to do to keep from being bored!

Your flesh may recoil from doing constructive things, but afterward you'll feel like a champion! Knowing you didn't go into more debt for more stuff you don't need will be so encouraging. You'll be so thankful you didn't waste your precious time doing things that don't matter. And you'll feel victorious for accomplishing something that has needed your attention for a very long time!

STUDY QUESTIONS

Study to shew thyself approved unto God, a workman that needeth not to be ashamed, rightly dividing the word of truth.
— 2 Timothy 2:15

1. In the days in which we live, there are many crazy, unprecedented things happening all around us. In what ways have you seen *envyings, murders, drunkenness,* and *revellings* play out in the public arena? How has it affected the quality of life?

2. One of the greatest gifts we can ask the Holy Spirit to cultivate in our lives and the lives of our children is *contentment.* As you carefully reflect on Paul's words in First Timothy 6:6-11, what is the Lord showing you to help you avoid the trap of greed, envy, and covetousness? (Also consider Proverbs 15:16,17; Luke 3:10-14; Hebrews 13:5.)

3. Instead of being drunk with wine, Paul said, "...Ever be filled and stimulated with the [Holy] Spirit" (Ephesians 5:18 *AMPC*). According to Jude 20 and First Corinthians 14:4, what happens to you when you pray in the heavenly language of the Spirit? How has being filled with the Spirit brought strength and encouragement in your life?

PRACTICAL APPLICATION

But be ye doers of the word, and not hearers only, deceiving your own selves.
— James 1:22

1. Do you have strong, hostile feelings toward someone because they seem to have an advantage or benefits that you want for yourself? If so, who are you envying, and what is it about their life that you want? Is your envy growing? Are you secretly hoping or scheming for something to happen to this person that would cause them to be demoted and you promoted? What immediate action do you know you need to take to escape this deadly snare of the flesh?

2. Have you ever personally seen the devastating effects of *drunkenness*? How has this work of the flesh left its mark on your family and friends? What might you share with others to urge them not to fall victim to the dangers of intoxication?

3. Take a few moments to reread the section on "Revellings." Prior to this lesson, had you ever heard of such things? In what ways can you see this fleshly behavior at work in the Church? How about in *you*? Are you struggling in any way with a consuming desire to be entertained or experience pleasure? What do you feel the Holy Spirit is prompting you to do to seize the time you've been given and put it to good use? (*See* Ephesians 5:14-17.)

LESSON 7

TOPIC

The Fruit of the Spirit

SCRIPTURES

1. **Galatians 5:16** — This I say then, Walk in the Spirit, and ye shall not fulfil the lust of the flesh.

2. **Galatians 5:19-21** — Now the works of the flesh are manifest, which are these; Adultery, fornication, uncleanness, lasciviousness, idolatry, witchcraft, hatred, variance, emulations, wrath, strife, seditions, heresies, envyings, murders, drunkenness, revellings, and such like....

3. **Galatians 5:22,23** — But the fruit of the Spirit is love, joy, peace, longsuffering, gentleness, goodness, faith, meekness, temperance; against such there is no law.

4. **Genesis 1:11,12** — And God said, Let the earth bring forth grass, the herb yielding seed, and the fruit tree yielding fruit after his kind, whose seed is in itself, upon the earth: and it was so. And the earth brought forth grass, and herb yielding seed after his kind, and the tree yielding fruit, whose seed was in itself, after his kind: and God saw that it was good.

5. **1 Peter 1:23** — Being born again, not of corruptible seed, but of incorruptible, by the word of God, which liveth and abideth for ever.

6. **1 John 3:9** — Whosoever is born of God doth not commit sin; for his seed remaineth in him: and he cannot sin, because he is born of God.

GREEK WORDS

1. "this I say" — **Λέγω δέ** (*Lego de*): I say categorically; I say emphatically

2. "walk" — **περιπατέω** (*peripateo*): a compound of the words **περι** (*peri*) and **πατέω** (*pateo*); the word **περι** (*peri*) means around and suggests the idea of something that is encircling; the word **πατέω** (*pateo*) means to walk and it denotes the movement of the feet; when compounded, to habitually walk around in one general vicinity; thus this word **περιπατέω** (*peripateo*) was often translated as the word 'live'

3. "shall not" — **οὐ μὴ** (*ou me*): the word **οὐ** (*ou*) is an emphatic no, with **μὴ** (*me*) which means no; you emphatically will not

4. "lust" — **ἐπιθυμία** (*epithumia*): from **ἐπί** (*epi*) and **θυμός** (*thumos*); the word **ἐπί** (*epi*) means over and gives intensity to the word; the word **θυμός** (*thumos*) is passionate desire; when these words are compounded to form **ἐπιθυμία** (*epithumia*), it describes desire, cravings, or carnal longings of the flesh; one bent over and craving a thing

5. "flesh" — **σαρκός** (*sarkos*): flesh; carnal nature; base fleshly instincts

6. "fruit" — **καρπός** (*karpos*): the fruit of plants, the fruit of trees, the fruit of one's body, such as a person's children or offspring

7. "seed" — **σπέρμα** (*sperma*): seed; sperm

SYNOPSIS

Imagine a delicious, mouthwatering meal — one that infuses you with health, strength, energy, and vitality. Can you smell the aroma? Can you taste the flavor? The zest is exploding in your mouth, providing all the vital nutrients your body needs to be vibrant, energized, and radiant with life.

That's the kind of spiritual food God longs to produce in the soil of your soul and spirit. He has planted the seed of His Spirit and His Word into your heart, and within His Seed is His divine DNA. All that God is — all His character and all His power — is ready to be reproduced in and through your life. But in order for you to experience an unending harvest of the fruit of the Spirit, you must learn to *walk in the Spirit* so that you don't fulfill the lust of your flesh.

The emphasis of this lesson:

Unlike a life controlled by the flesh, a life dominated by the Holy Spirit is filled with benefits and blessings! The moment we're born again, the divine Seed of God is implanted in us, and as we nurture that Seed, God's Spirit produces the fruit of love, joy, peace, longsuffering, gentleness, goodness, faith, meekness, and temperance in our lives.

A SYNOPSIS OF OUR ANCHOR VERSE
Galatians 5:16

Looking at our anchor verse once more, it says, "This I say then, Walk in the Spirit, and ye shall not fulfill the lust of the flesh" (Galatians 5:16). Here, we see the words "this I say," which in Greek is *Lego de*. The word *Lego* means *I say*, which is very strong on its own. To add even more strength, Paul inserted the little word *de*, which describes something that is *absolute*, *categorical*, or *emphatic*. With this in mind, we could translate the opening part of Galatians 5:16 to say:

> **Hear me! Hear what I'm saying to you! I'm telling you emphatically and with absolute certainty....**

What is Paul speaking about so categorically? He said, "...Walk in the Spirit, and ye shall not fulfill the lust of the flesh" (Galatians 5:16). We have established that this word "walk" doesn't describe a haphazard or accidental visit or a once-a-week requirement on Sundays to be spiritual. This word "walk" is the Greek word *peripateo*, which is a compound of the words *peri* and *pateo*. The word *peri* means *around* and signifies something that is *encircling*, and the word *pateo* comes from the Greek word meaning *to walk*. When these two words are joined to form the word *peripateo*, it depicts *one who habitually walks around in one general vicinity all the time*. This individual has walked and walked in one realm for so long it has become their place of existence. Therefore, we could translate this verse:

> **This I say to you emphatically, categorically, and with absolute certainty. If you habitually and continually walk and live in the Spirit, you shall not fulfill the lust of the flesh.**

We've seen that the words "shall not" in Greek are *ou me*. The word *ou* is emphatic for *no*, and the word *me* also means *no*. These words together form a double negative that literally means, *"You emphatically will not, in no way, fulfill the lust of the flesh."* In Greek, the word "flesh" here is *sarkos*, and it describes *the flesh; carnal nature;* or *base, fleshly instincts.* In Ephesians 2:3, Paul states that the flesh itself has desires, lusts, and a mind of its own. Therefore, to defeat the flesh, you must consistently say *no* to the flesh — you must deny it the opportunity to operate and say *yes* to the Spirit. If you will step up onto this high road of righteousness and begin to live in the realm of the Spirit, you will effectively pull the plug on the flesh.

Taking into account the original Greek meaning of the key words in this verse, here is the *Renner Interpretive Version (RIV)* of Galatians 5:16:

> **Make the path of the Spirit the place where you habitually live and walk. Become so comfortable on this spiritual path that you learn to leisurely and peacefully stroll along in that realm. Living your life in this Spirit realm is the best way to guarantee that you will not allow the yearnings of your flesh to creep out and fulfill themselves.**

In Galatians 5:19, the apostle Paul continues by saying, "Now the works of the flesh are manifest...." We've seen that the word "works" here is the Greek word *erga*, which describes *hard labor* or *hard work.* Without a doubt, what the flesh produces is *hard, demanding,* and *exhausting.* Specifically, the Bible says the works of the flesh are: "...Adultery, fornication, uncleanness, lasciviousness, idolatry, witchcraft, hatred, variance, emulations, wrath, strife, seditions, heresies, envyings, murders, drunkenness, revellings, and such like..." (Galatians 5:19-21).

For a detailed review of the meaning of each of these works, please refer back to Lessons 3, 4, 5, and 6.

The Spirit Produces Great 'Fruit'

When we come to Galatians 5:22 and 23, we discover what happens when we choose to walk and live in the realm of the Spirit. Paul wrote,

> **But the fruit of the Spirit is love, joy, peace, longsuffering, gentleness, goodness, faith, meekness, temperance; against such there is no law.**

Rick tells a story about what happened when he and Denise visited with a precious family who lived in a village in the Ukraine. When they arrived, they could see a huge table set up outside the house under a beautiful veranda, and the veranda was covered with luscious green vines laden with the biggest grapes they had ever seen anywhere in the world.

As the Renners sat and gazed at the vine, they noticed it was loaded with green, white, red, and purple grapes — many kinds of grapes they had never seen before. After they enjoyed a scrumptious lunch, it was time for dessert. But instead of ice cream or cake, their hosts brought out huge, oversized platters overflowing with plump, colorful grapes and placed them on the table right in front of them.

After Rick and Denise examined the grapes up close in amazement, they finally put them in their mouths and bit down. Suddenly, their mouths were bursting with rich flavor as the juices began to flow. It was the sweetest fruit they had ever tasted in their lives!

Indeed, fresh fruit is wonderful! It is healthy, beneficial, and delicious. This is one reason the apostle Paul used the word "fruit" to describe the wonderful things the Holy Spirit wants to produce inside our lives! Again, he said,

> **But the fruit of the Spirit is love, joy, peace, longsuffering, gentleness, goodness, faith, meekness, temperance; against such there is no law.**

Wow! What a contrast between the flesh and the Spirit! The flesh produces "works," which implies hard work and great exertion. A life dominated by the flesh is one filled with excess, imbalance, unhealthy extremes, laziness, self-abuse, hatred, strife, bitterness, irresponsibility, and neglect. It is the hardest route for any individual, yet the flesh still cries out to be in charge!

On the contrary, a life dominated by the Holy Spirit is filled with *benefits* and *blessings!* The apostle Paul likened these to "fruit." In Greek, this is the word *karpos*, and it describes *the fruit of plants*, *the fruit of trees*, and *the fruit of one's body*, such as a person's children or offspring.

But regardless of whether it is the fruit of a plant, an animal, or a human, all fruit is produced from some kind of *seed*. If there is no seed, there is no fruit. In fact, it is the seed that determines the fruit that will be produced. When God was creating the heavens and the earth, the Bible says:

> **And God said, Let the earth bring forth grass, the herb yielding *seed*, and the fruit tree yielding fruit after his kind, whose *seed***

is in itself, upon the earth: and it was so. And the earth brought forth grass, and herb yielding *seed* after his kind, and the tree yielding fruit, whose *seed* was in itself, after his kind: and God saw that it was good.

— **Genesis 1:11,12**

Again and again we see that *the seed produces its own kind*. That's why apples always produce apples, oranges always produce oranges, dogs always produce dogs, cats always produce cats, and humans always produce humans. The seed determines the fruit.

What Happens When We Are Born Again?

When the Holy Spirit moves upon a person's life and births them into the family of God, we say that he or she is *born again*. In that moment, the Bible says, "[We are] being born again, not of corruptible seed, but of incorruptible, by the word of God, which liveth and abideth for ever" (1 Peter 1:23). The moment you received Jesus as your Savior by faith, God planted His Spirit and Word into your heart *like a seed*. Instantly, you were born again by the incorruptible Word of God!

First John 3:9 confirms this saying, "Whosoever is born of God doth not commit sin; for his seed remaineth in him: and he cannot sin, because he is born of God." The word "seed" in this verse is the Greek word *sperma*, which means *seed* or *sperm*. This means God's divine sperm was injected into your spirit the very moment you were born again. In that Seed is the DNA of Almighty God — containing all aspects of God's power and the fruit of His Holy Spirit in spiritual-seed form.

Just as apples always produce apples and oranges always produce oranges, God's Seed in you will always produce God's character in your life! Hence, you should expect to produce the fruit of the Spirit in your life. Because God's Seed is inside you, it is natural for you to produce the life and character of God in your life.

Does a vinedresser worry that his grapevines will produce oranges? No! Does the owner of an orange grove run to the orchard to see if his trees are producing watermelons? Of course not! Every seed always produces after its own kind, and this same principle holds true in the spiritual realm. If God has planted His Spirit into your heart, you have every right to expect God's divine fruit to be reproduced in your life!

The fruit the Spirit produces is wonderful, godly fruit, overflowing with blessings and life. And once others partake of the love, joy, peace, long-suffering, gentleness, goodness, faith, meekness, and temperance that is evident in your life, they will want to come back for multiple servings of that luscious fruit!

You'll leave a good taste in people's mouths, and as a result you'll leave them wanting more. So don't give way to the flesh and allow it to produce its ugly work in your life. Instead, yield to the Spirit and allow the seed of God's Spirit and Word to produce the fruit of the Spirit in your life.

The Choice Is Yours!

God says, "…I have set before you life and death, blessing and cursing; therefore choose life, that both you and your descendants may live" (Deuteronomy 30:19 *NKJV*). How can you choose life? Obey God's command spoken through the apostle Paul: **"This I say then, Walk in the Spirit, and ye shall not fulfill the lust of the flesh" (Galatians 5:16).**

Again, "walk" — the Greek word *peripateo* — is not an occasional, hit and miss visit. To walk in the Spirit is to *live* in the Spirit. The word *peripateo* depicts *one who habitually walks around in one general vicinity all the time*. Thus, the path of the Spirit is his life — it's the only path he knows. This means you can live in the Spirit, and as you do you will not fulfill the lust of the flesh.

Remember, the word "lust" is the Greek word *epithumia*, which is a compound of the words *epi* and *thumos*. The word *epi* means *over* and is an intensifying term, and the word *thumos* describes *passionate desire*. When these words are compounded to form *epithumia*, it describes *desire, cravings, or carnal longings of the flesh*. It pictures someone doubled over having withdrawals, hankering and hungering for something desperately.

Paul says these carnal cravings and longings are of the "flesh," which depicts *the carnal nature* and *base, fleshly instincts*. If you don't put the flesh to death by the power of the Holy Spirit, it will go to work producing harsh and painful consequences in your life. However, if you choose to live in the Spirit, you will effectively pull the plug on the flesh.

So what do you want? You can choose the cruel, hard, bitter works of the flesh:

...Adultery, fornication, uncleanness, lasciviousness, idolatry, witchcraft, hatred, variance, emulations, wrath, strife, seditions, heresies, envyings, murders, drunkenness, revellings, and such like... (Galatians 5:19-21).

Or you can partake of the supernatural, life-giving fruits of the Spirit:

...Love, joy, peace, longsuffering, gentleness, goodness, faith, meekness, [and] temperance... (Galatians 5:22,23).

Friend, choose the high road — choose to walk in the Spirit and you will not fulfill the lust of the flesh. In our next lesson, we will begin to explore the meaning of the first and most important fruit of the Spirit — the fruit of *love*.

STUDY QUESTIONS

> Study to shew thyself approved unto God, a workman that needeth
> not to be ashamed, rightly dividing the word of truth.
> — 2 Timothy 2:15

1. The moment you received Jesus as your Lord and Savior, God planted His Spirit and Word into your heart like a *seed*. Instantly, you were born again by the incorruptible Word of God! According to John 1:1-4, who is the Word? What part did the Word play in creation? (Also consider Colossians 1:15-17.) Knowing that the "Word" has been deposited within you, what good things are you expecting — and asking — Him to create in and through your life?

2. It's interesting to note that immediately after listing all the fruit of the Spirit that God wants to produce in our lives, the Bible says, "Those who belong to Christ Jesus have nailed the passions and desires of their sinful nature to his cross and crucified them there. Since we are living by the Spirit, let us follow the Spirit's leading in every part of our lives" (Galatians 5:24,25 *NLT*). What can you do differently to ensure that your flesh stays crucified with Christ every day? (Consider Romans 8:13; Philippians 4:13; Galatians 2:20; and Second Corinthians 9:8 and use them to create a personal prayer of dedication to God, asking Him for His grace to live in the Spirit.)

PRACTICAL APPLICATION

**But be ye doers of the word, and not hearers only,
deceiving your own selves.
— James 1:22**

1. Since God has planted His Spirit into your heart, you have every right to expect the divine fruit of the Spirit to be reproduced in your life! The question is, *are you expecting it?* Are you believing for and anticipating things like love, joy, peace, patience, and kindness to burst forth in your life? If not, why?

2. Who do you know that is producing the fruit of the Spirit in their life? What specific fruits (qualities of Christ) have you sampled and enjoyed from them? How have these godly fruits nourished your life? Have you gone back for multiple servings of that luscious fruit?

3. God's Word says, "O taste and see that the Lord is good... (Psalm 34:8)," and that "...We are Christ's ambassadors; God is making his appeal through us..." (2 Corinthians 5:20 *NLT*). Take a moment and pray: *Lord, what kind of taste am I leaving in people's mouths? Does my life make You appealing to others or repulsive? If I wasn't a Christian and I was around someone just like me, would I be attracted to Jesus or repelled?*

LESSON 8

TOPIC

The First Fruit

SCRIPTURES

1. **Galatians 5:16** — This I say then, Walk in the Spirit, and ye shall not fulfil the lust of the flesh

2. **Galatians 5:19-21** — Now the works of the flesh are manifest, which are these; Adultery, fornication, uncleanness, lasciviousness, idolatry, witchcraft, hatred, variance, emulations, wrath, strife, seditions, heresies, envyings, murders, drunkenness, revellings, and such like....

3. **Galatians 5:22,23** — But the fruit of the Spirit is love, joy, peace, longsuffering, gentleness, goodness, faith, meekness, temperance; against such there is no law.

4. **John 3:16** — For God so loved the world, that he gave his only begotten Son, that whosoever believeth in him should not perish, but have everlasting life.

5. **1 John 3:16** — Hereby perceive we the love of God, because he laid down his life for us: and we ought to lay down our lives for the brethren.

6. **1 John 3:18** — My little children, let us not love in word, neither in tongue; but in deed and in truth.

7. **1 Corinthians 14:1** — Follow after charity [agape love]....

GREEK WORDS

1. "this I say" — **Λέγω δέ** (*Lego de*): I say categorically; I say emphatically

2. "walk" — **περιπατέω** (*peripateo*): a compound of the words **περι** (*peri*) and **πατέω** (*pateo*); the word **περι** (*peri*) means *around* and suggests the idea of something that is encircling; the word **πατέω** (*pateo*) means *to walk* and denotes the movement of the feet; when compounded, to habitually walk around in one general vicinity; thus this word **περιπατέω** (*peripateo*) was often translated as the word "live"

3. "shall not" — **οὐ μὴ** (*ou me*): the word **οὐ** (*ou*) is an emphatic *no*; but with **μὴ** (*me*), which simply means *no, you emphatically will not*

4. "flesh" — **σαρκός** (*sarkos*): flesh; carnal nature; base fleshly instincts

5. "fruit" — **καρπός** (*karpos*): the fruit of plants, the fruit of trees, the fruit of one's body, such as a person's children or offspring

6. "love" — (*agape*): *Agape* occurs when an individual sees, recognizes, understands, or appreciates the value of an object or a person, causing the viewer to behold that object or person in great esteem, awe, admiration, wonder, and sincere appreciation. Such great respect is awakened in the heart of the observer for the object or person he is beholding that he is compelled to love it. In fact, his love for that person or object is so strong that it is irresistible. *Agape* is a love that loves so profoundly that it knows no limits or boundaries in how far, wide, high, and deep it will go to show that love to its recipient. If necessary, agape love will even sacrifice itself for the sake of that object or person it so deeply cherishes. Agape is the highest form of love — a self-sacrificial type of love that moves the lover to action.

SYNOPSIS

If there was ever an aspect of God's character we can always use more revelation on, it is His *love*. His love is so deep and so wide that there are always new facets to discover in our daily walk with Him.

As you dive into this lesson on God's *agape* love — which is the first fruit of the Holy Spirit listed in Galatians 5:22 — we pray for you as the apostle Paul prayed for the Ephesian believers: "…May your roots go down deep into the soil of God's marvelous love; and may you be able to feel and understand, as all God's children should, how long, how wide, how deep, and how high his love really is; and to experience this love for yourselves…" (Ephesians 3:17-19 *TLB*).

The emphasis of this lesson:

The four primary Greek words to describe the concept of love are *eros*, *stergo*, *phileo*, and *agape*. The highest form of love is *agape*, which is the love of God and a fruit of the Spirit. *Agape* has no limits on how far it will go to show love to its recipient. It is unconditional, self-sacrificing, and pure. It is demonstrated through action and expects nothing in return.

A REVIEW OF OUR ANCHOR VERSE
Galatians 5:16

Since repetition is one of the greatest teachers, let's briefly go over our anchor verse again. Speaking to the believers in Galatia, Paul said, "This I say then, Walk in the Spirit, and ye shall not fulfill the lust of the flesh" (Galatians 5:16). When Paul says, "This I say," he uses the Greek words *Lego de*, which is a strong statement. The word *Lego* means *I say*, and the little word *de* intensifies the meaning, making Paul's words even more forceful. This word *de* describes something that is *absolute*, *indisputable*, or *emphatic*. Hence, we could translate the opening part of this verse to say:

> **"Now hear me! I'm telling you indisputably and emphatically and with absolute certainty…."**

What is Paul telling us so strongly? He said, "…Walk in the Spirit, and ye shall not fulfill the lust of the flesh" (Galatians 5:16). In Greek, the word "walk" is the word *peripateo*, which is a compound of the words *peri* and *pateo*. The word *peri* means *around* and indicates something that is *encircling*, and the word *pateo* means *to walk*. When these words are joined to form the word *peripateo*, it pictures *one who habitually walks around in one general vicinity all the time*. This lets us know that walking in the Spirit is not something we do occasionally. It is something we should do — and *can* do — regularly. If God has called us to habitually walk and live in the Spirit, it is something that is attainable.

What happens when you regularly walk in the Spirit? Paul said, "...Ye shall not fulfill the lust of the flesh" (Galatians 5:16). This means living in the realm of the Spirit is the guaranteed way to make sure you don't gratify and satisfy the yearnings of the flesh. The word "flesh" in this verse is the Greek word *sarkos*, and it describes *the carnal nature* or *base fleshly instincts*.

Taking into account the original Greek meaning of the key words in this verse, here is the *Renner Interpretive Version* (*RIV*) of Galatians 5:16:

> **Make the path of the Spirit the place where you habitually live and walk. Become so comfortable on this spiritual path that you learn to leisurely and peacefully stroll along in that realm. Living your life in this Spirit realm is the best way to guarantee that you will not allow the yearnings of your flesh to creep out and fulfill themselves.**

What Are the Works of the Flesh?

Paul tells us in Galatians 5:19-21, "Now the works of the flesh are manifest, which are these; Adultery, fornication, uncleanness, lasciviousness, idolatry, witchcraft, hatred, variance, emulations, wrath, strife, seditions, heresies, envyings, murders, drunkenness, revellings, and such like...." These are the kinds of hard, troublesome, and demanding consequences of letting your flesh control you. (For a detailed review of the meaning of each of these works, please refer to Lessons 3-6.)

What Are the Fruit of the Spirit?

Thankfully, God has given us a positive alternative to following after the flesh and producing its destructive works. That alternative is called *walking in the Spirit*, and when we walk in the Spirit, the Spirit produces wonderful, life-giving fruit in our lives, including, "...Love, joy, peace, longsuffering, gentleness, goodness, faith, meekness, temperance…." And we know that "…against such there is no law." (*See* Galatians 5:22,23.)

The reason we are able to produce such godly fruit is because the divine Seed of Almighty God has been planted in us in the new birth. The Bible says, "You have been regenerated (born again), not from a mortal origin (seed, sperm), but from one that is immortal by the ever living and lasting Word of God" (1 Peter 1:23 *AMPC*).

When we call on the name of Jesus Christ and make Him the Lord of our lives, the Holy Spirit comes into our spirit and brings the Seed of God into us. Spiritually speaking, the divine DNA of God — which carries all the life, power, and nature of God — is injected into our human spirits the moment we're born again. Therefore, all of God is resident inside of you in seed form if you've been born again. And just like apple seeds produce apples and orange seeds produce oranges, God's Seed produces the life of God in your life. The evidence of this is seen in the fruit of the Spirit being produced in our lives subsequent to our experiencing the new birth.

There Are Four Types of Love

When the New Testament was being written during the First Century, there were four primary Greek words to describe the concept of love. These include *eros, stergo, phileo,* and *agape.* These four words conveyed four very different types of love.

#1: Eros

The first word for "love" is the Greek word *eros.* It is the Greek term for *sexual love* and it's where we get the word "erotic." In Greek culture, this word referred to sensual, carnal impulses to satisfy or gratify the sexual desires of the flesh. It shares a root with the word *erao,* which means *to ask, to beg,* or *to demand.* Hence, it usually denotes a sexual demand.

This means *eros* is not a giving type of love. It is a carnal love primarily focused on the fulfillment of its own desires. This low-level love thinks about itself and what it can get and how good it can feel — not what it can give to others.

Because the word *eros* primarily describes a *self-satisfying, self-gratifying, self-seeking, self-pleasing* type of sexual appetite, it is not the type of love that believers should aspire to — even in their marital lives. Throughout the New Testament, regardless of whether the context is friendship, brotherhood, or romance, all believers are urged to operate from the perspective of *agape* love — a higher love more focused on giving than on receiving.

#2: Stergo

The second word for "love" is the Greek word *stergo*, and it primarily pictures *a love that exists between parents and children* or *a love between members of a family*. One scholar has noted that the word *stergo* portrayed the love of a nation for its ruler or even the love of a dog for its master. Consequently, the real idea of the word *stergo* is that of *devotion*.

This word rarely appears in the New Testament except for an occasional mention, such as its appearance in Second Timothy 3:3, where the apostle Paul says that people in the last days will be, "Without natural affection...." Here it is used in a negative sense to forecast the deterioration of strong family ties and devotion to one's family in the last days.

3: Phileo

The third word for "love" is the Greek word *phileo*, which describes *affection* such as *the affection felt between a boyfriend and girlfriend* or *affection shared between two friends*. It carries the idea of two or more people who feel compatible, well-matched, well-suited, and complementary to each other.

Although this is a higher form of love than *eros*, it is still not as high as *agape*. *Phileo* love is based on mutual satisfaction, which means if one person suddenly doesn't feel loved by the other, this love can be lost.

Other words derived from the word *phileo* are numerous. They include words like *philedelphia*, meaning brotherly love; *philanthropia*, meaning *one who loves or who is kind to mankind*; and *philosophia*, meaning *a love of wisdom*.

#4: Agape

The fourth word for "love" used in the First Century is the word *agape*, and it is chiefly used in the New Testament to depict *the love of God*. It is the highest level of love known, and it is the very word Paul used for "love" in Galatians 5:22 when he wrote: "But the fruit of the Spirit is *love*...."

There is no love higher, finer, or more excellent than *agape* love. In fact, the word *agape* is so filled with deep emotion and meaning that it is one of the most difficult words to translate in the New Testament. Trying to explain this word has baffled translators for centuries. Nevertheless, using all that is available to us, here is what we understand the meaning of this powerful word to be.

Agape love occurs when an individual sees, recognizes, understands, or appreciates the value of an object or a person, causing the viewer to behold that object or person in great esteem, awe, admiration, wonder, and sincere appreciation. Such great respect is awakened in the heart of the observer for the object or person he is beholding that he is compelled to love it. In fact, his love for that person or object is so strong that it is irresistible.

The Greatest Display of *Agape*

In the New Testament, perhaps the best example of *agape* is found in the words of Jesus recorded in John 3:16:

> **For God so loved the world, that he gave his only begotten Son, that whosoever believeth in him should not perish, but have everlasting life.**

In the phrase, "For God so loved the world," the word "love" is the Greek word *agape*. This means when God looked upon the human race, He stood in awe of mankind, even though man was lost in sin. God admired man; He wondered at man; and He held mankind in the highest appreciation.

Even though mankind was held captive by Satan at that moment, God looked upon the world and saw His own image in man. The human race was so precious to God and He loved man so deeply that His heart was stirred to reach out and to do something to save him. In other words, God's love drove Him to action.

You see, *agape* is a love that loves so profoundly that it knows no limits or boundaries in how far, wide, high, and deep it will go to show that love to its recipient. If necessary, *agape* love will even sacrifice itself for the sake of that object or person it so deeply cherishes. *Agape* is the highest form of love — a self-sacrificial type of love that moves the lover to action. In contrast:

- *Eros* is a self-seeking love.

- *Stergo* is limited only to one's family; it is very restricted.

- *Phileo* is based on mutual satisfaction and can feel disappointed and can wane.

Agape is a love that has no strings attached. It isn't looking for what it can get, but for what it can *give*. Its awe of the one who is loved is so deep that it is compelled to shower love upon that object or person regardless of the response. This is the profound love God has for the human race, for He loved man when man was lost in sin with no ability to love Him back. God simply loved mankind without any thought or expectation of receiving love in return.

When you love with such a pure love that you expect nothing in return, it is impossible to feel hurt or let down by the response of the recipients. You don't love them for the purpose of getting something in return. You shower them with love simply because you love them. This kind of love is much higher than *eros* love that is based on selfishness; *stergo* love that is restricted by limitations; and *phileo* love that is rooted in mutual satisfaction. These three types of love are low-level love, but *agape* is high-level love. It is a love that has no strings attached, a love that loves simply and purely — the God-kind of love.

As Believers, We Are Called to Walk in *Agape* Love

In First John 3:16, we are urged to possess *agape* for each other. Here John says, "Hereby perceive we the love of God, because he laid down his life for us: and we ought to lay down our lives for the brethren." This means we are to love and appreciate each other just as fully and freely as God loves us.

The Father loved us to the point of self-sacrifice. Jesus' *agape* drove Him to lay down His life for us. In the same way, we are to *agape* our brothers and sisters to such an extent that we would be willing to lay down our lives for them. If we are operating in *agape* and they don't respond in like fashion, it won't offend or disappoint us, because we are not looking for what others can do for us. We are simply focused on how to love others with no strings attached. Therefore, the way other people respond to us has no effect on our desire to shower them with *agape* love.

The apostle John continues to explain the role of *agape* in our lives by saying, "My little children, let us not love in word, neither in tongue; but in deed and in truth" (1 John 3:18). The word "love" here is again the Greek word *agape*, and it is telling us that *agape* love is not passive. Rather, it is actively demonstrating itself with deeds and actions ("in deed and in truth"). This is not an empty love that talks, but does nothing. It is a love that does something — just as God loved us and then did something to save us from our lost and sinful condition.

This is the love that Paul urged us to follow after when he wrote in First Corinthians 14:1, "Follow after charity [agape love]...." The word "follow" here is the Greek word *dioko*, which means *to hotly pursue*. The word *dioko* was a hunting term that pictured *a hunter following the tracks and scent of an animal until he finally captures what he's after*. This means that attaining this high-level love doesn't come easy. If we want to attain *agape* love and regularly walk in it, we must hotly pursue it! It must be the *focus* and the *aim* of our lives.

If *agape* is the basis of your sexual relationship with your spouse instead of *eros*, you will always seek to serve and to please your spouse rather than being self-centered and focused only on *your* needs. If *agape* is the basis of your family relationships rather than *stergo*, you will always remain devoted to your family, regardless of the disappointments that may occur along the way. And if *agape* is the basis of your friendships rather than *phileo*, you will be a faithful, immovable friend for life rather than a come-and-go friend who is faithful only as long as you get what you want out of the relationship.

In fact, if *agape* is the driving motivation of your life and the force behind all your relationships, it will empower you to be the best, most devoted, faithful, and reliable friend anyone has ever known.

You may ask, "But how can I possess such love? Is it really possible for me to regularly exhibit such love in my life for other people?" The answer is *yes*! When you walk in the Spirit, you will not gratify or satisfy the selfish cravings of your flesh. Instead, because the seed of God's Word has been sown into your own human spirit, the potential for you to flow in His divine *agape* love is within you all the time. If you'll let the Spirit of God release it from your heart, you will discover and enjoy the fruit of the Spirit called "love."

Now is the time for you to allow the Holy Spirit to manifest that fruit in your life!

STUDY QUESTIONS

Study to shew thyself approved unto God, a workman that needeth not to be ashamed, rightly dividing the word of truth.
— 2 Timothy 2:15

1. In your own words, briefly describe the four types of love, explaining which ones function in each of your relationships.
2. If you've ever wondered if God loves you, *He does!* How has He demonstrated His love for you? Look at what He says in First John 3:1,16; Romans 5:8; Ephesians 2:4,5; and Titus 3:3-7.
3. Paul paints a powerful picture of what *agape* love looks like in First Corinthians 13:4-8. Carefully read this passage in a few different Bible translations and identify the multiple ways *agape* love behaves. Keep in mind, these are the ways God personally loves *you*. As you receive His love, His Spirit enables you to love others in these same ways.

PRACTICAL APPLICATION

But be ye doers of the word, and not hearers only, deceiving your own selves.
— James 1:22

1. *Agape* is high-level love that has "no strings attached." It isn't looking for what it can get, but for what it can *give*. Who can you think of who has loved you with this God-kind of love? How did that person tangibly demonstrate this love to you, and what impact did it have on your life?
2. What would you say is one of the greatest examples in your life of God demonstrating His unconditional, *agape* love for you? How does His indescribable love for you motivate you to love others?
3. Just as God's *agape* love for us drove Him to action, His agape love *in* us should drive us to action toward others. First John 3:18 (*TLB*) says, "Let us stop just saying we love people; let us really love them, and show it by our actions." What are some of the ways you have tangibly

expressed God's love to others? Is there anything specific you sense
He is asking you to do for someone right now? If so, what is it?

TOPIC

Joy, Peace, Longsuffering, Gentleness

SCRIPTURES

1. **Galatians 5:16** — This I say then, Walk in the Spirit, and ye shall not
    fulfil the lust of the flesh.

2. **Galatians 5:19-21** — Now the works of the flesh are manifest, which
    are these; Adultery, fornication, uncleanness, lasciviousness, idolatry,
    witchcraft, hatred, variance, emulations, wrath, strife, seditions, here-
    sies, envyings, murders, drunkenness, revellings, and such like....

3. **Galatians 5:22,23** — But the fruit of the Spirit is love, joy, peace,
    longsuffering, gentleness, goodness, faith, meekness, temperance;
    against such there is no law.

4. **1 Thessalonians 1:6** — And ye became followers of us, and of the
    Lord, having received the word in much affliction, with joy of the
    Holy Ghost.

5. **Acts 27:22-24** — And now I exhort you to be of good cheer: for there
    shall be no loss of any man's life among you, but of the ship. For there
    stood by me this night the angel of God, whose I am, and whom I
    serve, saying, Fear not...

6. **1 Corinthians 13:4** — Charity [or love] suffereth long....

7. **1 Corinthians 9:20-22** — And unto the Jews I became as a Jew, that
    I might gain the Jews; to them that are under the law, as under the
    law, that I might gain them that are under the law; to them that are
    without law, as without law, (being not without law to God, but under
    the law to Christ,) that I might gain them that are that are without
    the law. To the weak became I as weak, that I might gain the weak: I
    am made all things to all men, that I might by all means save some."

GREEK WORDS

1. "this I say" — **Λέγω δέ** (*Lego de*): I say categorically; I say emphatically

2. "walk" — **περιπατέω** (*peripateo*): a compound of the words **περι** (*peri*) and **πατέω** (*pateo*); the word **περι** (*peri*) means *around* and suggests the idea of something that is encircling; the word **πατέω** (*pateo*) means *to walk* and denotes the movement of the feet; when compounded, to habitually walk around in one general vicinity; thus this word **περιπατέω** (*peripateo*) was often translated as the word "live"

3. "shall not" — **οὐ μὴ** (*ou me*): the word **οὐ** (*ou*) is an emphatic *no*; but with **μὴ** (*me*), which simply means *no*, it means *you emphatically will not*

4. "fruit" — **καρπός** (*karpos*): the fruit of plants, the fruit of trees, the fruit of one's body, such as a person's children or offspring

5. "joy" — **χαρά** (*chara*) from **χάρις** (*charis*): grace-produced; joy is divine in origin; someone may feel happiness, merriment, hilarity, exuberance, excitement, or be in high spirits, but all of these express fleeting emotions; joy on the other hand is a grace-produced expression that flourishes even when times are strenuous, daunting, or tough

6. "affliction" — **θλῖψις** (*thlipsis*): great pressure; crushing pressure; to suffocate; to bully; the brunt of society; pressure to conform; a horribly tight, life-threatening squeeze; a situation so difficult it caused one to feel stressed, squeezed, pressured, or crushed

7. "peace" — **εἰρήνη** (*eirene*): the cessation of war; conflict that's put away; a time of rebuilding and reconstruction after war has ceased; distractions removed; a time of prosperity; the rule of order in the place of chaos; a calm, inner stability that results in the ability to conduct oneself peacefully even in the midst of circumstances that would normally be traumatic or upsetting; the Greek equivalent for the Hebrew word *shalom*, which expresses the idea of wholeness, completeness or tranquility in the soul that is unaffected by outward circumstances or pressures

8. "longsuffering" — **μακροθυμία** (*makrothumia*): compound of **μακρός** (*makros*) and **θυμός** (*thumos*); the word **μακρός** (*makros*): means long, and **θυμός** (*thumos*) depicts a passionate desire; compounded, it is a long-held passion; the patient restraint of anger and therefore long-suffering; can be translated as the words "forbearance" or "patience"; it

is ready to forbear and patiently wait; it doesn't easily give up or bow out

9. "gentleness" — χρηστότης (*chrestotes*): pictures one who is adaptable to others; a person with this trait seeks to become adaptable to the needs of those who are around him

SYNOPSIS

Being attractive is a top priority to many people. It's why Americans spent more than 49 billion dollars on cosmetics and more than 32 billion dollars on perfumes and colognes in 2019 alone. Unfortunately, makeup and fragrances only bring temporary change to our outward appearance.

If we really want to become attractive to people, the real key lies in cultivating the fruit of the Spirit. People are starving for *love* and *peace* — not to mention *joy, gentleness*, and *goodness*. When our lives begin to produce a sweet harvest of these types of godly fruit and people get a taste of it, they will naturally be drawn to us. How do we yield such satisfying sustenance? The answer is *by walking in the Spirit*.

The emphasis of this lesson:

Joy **is contentment produced by God's grace that is unaffected by outward circumstances. Similarly,** *peace* **is divine inner stability and calmness of the soul that is impervious to external forces. The fruit of** *longsuffering* **is the supernatural ability to restrain anger and be patient. And** *gentleness* **is the divine ability to be kind and adaptable to others.**

A REVIEW OF OUR ANCHOR VERSE

Galatians 5:16

Have you ever said to yourself, *Man, I wish I knew what I could do to get a handle on what I'm doing. I just seem to be out of control.* Well, the apostle Paul answers this question in Galatians 5:16 by saying, "This I say then, Walk in the Spirit, and ye shall not fulfill the lust of the flesh." (Galatians 5:16). In Greek, the phrase "this I say" is *Lego de*, which is a strong statement. The word *Lego* means *I say*, and the word *de* intensifies the meaning even more. This word *de* describes something that is *absolute, indisputable,* or *categorical*. It is as if Paul was raising his voice and saying:

"Hear me and hear me well! I'm telling you indisputably, emphatically, and categorically…"

What was Paul saying so forcefully? He said, "…Walk in the Spirit, and ye shall not fulfill the lust of the flesh" (Galatians 5:16). We have seen that the Greek word for "walk" here is *peripateo*, which is a compound of the words *peri* and *pateo*. The word *peri* means *around* and indicates something that is *encircling*, and the word *pateo* means *to walk*. When these words are compounded to form the word *peripateo*, it depicts *one who habitually walks around in one general vicinity all the time.*

The use of the word *peripateo* ("walk") tells us that walking in the Spirit is *living* in the Spirit. Thus, God doesn't want us to occasionally visit His presence — He wants His presence to be the realm where we habitually live our lives. Why? Because when we consistently live in the Spirit, Paul said, "…Ye shall not fulfill the lust of the flesh" (Galatians 5:16). We've seen that the words "shall not" in Greek are *ou mé*, which together form a double negative that literally means, *"You absolutely will not, in no way, fulfill the lust of the flesh."*

Taking into account the original Greek meaning of the key words in this verse, here is the *Renner Interpretive Version* (*RIV*) of Galatians 5:16:

> **Make the path of the Spirit the place where you habitually live and walk. Become so comfortable on this spiritual path that you learn to leisurely and peacefully stroll along in that realm. Living your life in this Spirit realm is the best way to guarantee that you will not allow the yearnings of your flesh to creep out and fulfill themselves.**

This verse clearly tells us that we have a *choice* that is always before us: We can either walk according to the demands and cravings of our fleshly carnal nature, or we can walk and live our lives following the leading of the Holy Spirit.

If We Follow the Flesh…

Paul tells us what kinds of things we can expect our lives to produce. He said, "Now the works of the flesh are manifest, which are these; Adultery, fornication, uncleanness, lasciviousness, idolatry, witchcraft, hatred, variance, emulations, wrath, strife, seditions, heresies, envyings, murders, drunkenness, revellings, and such like…" (Galatians 5:19-21). These are the *hard, wearisome* consequences of giving into your fleshly impulses. (For a detailed review of the meaning of each of these works, please refer to Lessons 3-6.)

But If We Follow the Spirit...

God guarantees we can avoid fulfilling the lust of the flesh. When we walk and live in the Spirit and cooperate with His direction, He will produce a harvest of wonderful fruit in our lives. Galatians 5:22 and 23 says, "But the fruit of the Spirit is love, joy, peace, longsuffering, gentleness, goodness, faith, meekness, temperance; against such there is no law."

In Greek, the word "fruit" here is *karpos*, which describes *the fruit of plants, the fruit of trees*, and *the fruit of one's body*, such as a person's children or offspring. All fruit is produced from some kind of *seed*. If there is no seed, there is no fruit. Indeed, it is the seed that determines the type of fruit that will be produced.

The reason we're able to bear such godly fruit as love, joy, and peace is because the divine Seed of Almighty God has been planted in us. The moment we turn to Jesus and repent of our sins, the Bible says, "...[We are] born again, not of corruptible seed but incorruptible, through the word of God which lives and abides forever" (1 Peter 1:23, *NKJV*).

The instant we get saved, the Holy Spirit comes into our spirit and brings the Seed of God into us. This Seed is the divine DNA of God, and it contains the spiritual genetic code that will replicate in us every detail of the life and nature of God. Therefore, all that God *is* takes up residence inside us in seed form. And just like apple seeds produce apples and orange seeds produce oranges, God's Seed will produce God's life in our life. The proof of the presence of the Seed is in the fruit we bear.

'Joy' Is Unaffected by Outward Circumstances

In our last lesson, we saw that the first fruit of the Spirit Paul listed is *love*. Next in line is "joy." Joy is not happiness by the world's standards. It is a much higher level of confident contentment. The word "joy" is the Greek word *chara*, which is from *charis*, the word for "grace." This tells us that joy is *grace-produced* and is *divine in origin*. Although someone may feel happiness, merriment, hilarity, exuberance, excitement, or be in high spirits, all of these are fleeting emotions. Genuine joy, on the other hand, is a grace-produced expression that flourishes even when times are strenuous, daunting, or tough.

An example of this "joy" is found in First Thessalonians 1:6, which says, "And ye became followers of us, and of the Lord, having received the word in much affliction, with joy of the Holy Ghost." First of all, notice that the joy mentioned here is *of the Holy Ghost*. That means the Holy Spirit produced it.

What is interesting here is that in the very same verse, we see that the believers were experiencing "affliction." In Greek, this is the word *thlipsis*, and it describes *great pressure* or *crushing pressure*. It is something that is *suffocating*. It can also mean *to bully* or experience *the brunt of society*. This word *thlipsis* indicates *a pressure to conform* and carries the idea of *a horribly tight, life-threatening squeeze*. It is a situation so difficult it causes one to feel *stressed*, *squeezed*, *pressured*, or *crushed*.

This word is so strong that it leaves no room for misunderstanding regarding the intensity of the afflictions the Thessalonians faced. The word *thlipsis* conveys the idea of *a heavy-pressure situation*. One scholar says it was used to describe the act of tying a victim with a rope, laying him on his back, and placing a huge boulder on top of him until his body was crushed. Paul used this word to alert his readers to moments when he or others went through grueling, crushing situations that would have been unbearable, intolerable, and impossible to survive if it had not been for the help of the Holy Spirit.

One of the ways the Holy Spirit helps is to give us supernatural *joy*. Again, it's important to understand that this divine joy isn't on the same level as mere happiness. Happiness is based on circumstantial pleasure, merriment, hilarity, exuberance, excitement, or something that causes one to feel hopeful or to be in high spirits. These fleeting emotions of happiness, although pleasurable at the moment, usually go just as quickly as they come. All it takes is one bit of bad news, a sour look from a fellow employee, a harsh word from a spouse, or an electric bill that is larger than what was anticipated — and that emotion of happiness can disappear right from before a person's eyes!

But joy is unaffected by outward circumstances. In fact, it usually thrives best when times are tough! It is God's supernatural response to the devil's attacks!

"Joy" — the Greek word *chara* — is produced by the *charis* ("grace") of God. This means "joy" isn't a human-based happiness that comes and goes. Rather, true "joy" is divine in origin and a fruit of the Spirit that is manifested and flourishes best particularly in hard, strenuous, and daunting times.

In the example given in First Thessalonians 1:6, the Thessalonians were under great stress due to persecution, but in the midst of it all, they continued to experience great joy. In fact, the Greek implies that their joy was due to the Spirit's work in them. Paul even called it the "joy of the Holy Ghost."

Taking into account the original Greek meaning of the key words in this verse, here is the *Renner Interpretive Version* (*RIV*) of First Thessalonians 1:6:

> **You threw your arms open wide and gladly welcomed the Word into your lives with great enthusiasm. And you did it even in the midst of mind-boggling sufferings — a level of stress and intensity that would be suffocating and crushing for most people. But while you were going through all these hardships and hassles, you were simultaneously experiencing the supreme joy of the Holy Spirit.**

The best the world has to offer is a temporary happiness. But when the seed of God has been placed inside your human spirit, His divine DNA produces a joy that isn't based on outward events or circumstances. In fact, when times get very challenging, the supernatural life of God rises up inside you to defy that devilish pressure! This supernatural joy will sustain you in even the hardest of times!

'Peace' Is Divine *Inner Stability* and *Calmness*

In addition to love and joy, Paul proclaimed that *peace* would also be produced in you by the Holy Spirit (*see* Galatians 5:22). The Greek word for "peace" here is *eirene*, which describes *the cessation of war* or *a conflict that has been put away*. It is a time of rebuilding and reconstruction after war has ceased; the distractions have been removed and a time of prosperity has set in.

This word *eirene* (peace) suggests *the rule of order in the place of chaos*. It is *a calm, inner stability that results in the ability to conduct oneself peacefully even in the midst of circumstances that would normally be traumatic or upsetting.* Interestingly, *eirene* is the Greek equivalent for the Hebrew word *shalom*, which expresses the idea of *wholeness, completeness,* or *tranquility in the soul that is unaffected by outward circumstances or pressures.*

The New Testament is filled with examples of this supernatural peace that the Holy Spirit produces. A great example is found in Acts 27 when the apostle Paul found himself in a ship that was being tossed back and forth by the raging waves of the sea. The storm was so intense and overwhelming that "...all hope that [they] should be saved was then taken away" (Acts 27:20).

But right in the midst of all this hopelessness, Paul stood up and said, "And now I exhort you to be of good cheer: for there shall be no loss of any man's life among you, but of the ship. For there stood by me this night the angel of God, whose I am, and whom I serve, saying, Fear not..." (Acts 27:22-24).

When Paul heard that word from the Lord, a supernatural peace rose up inside him, and he became like a rock in the middle of a very serious situation. His peace brought strength to everyone on that ship! And if you'll let the Holy Spirit work in you, He will release a supernatural, dominating peace from deep inside you. This fruit of the Spirit will keep you calm, stable, and peaceful, even if you are facing circumstances that would normally push you over the edge!

'Longsuffering' Is the Divine Ability To Be *Patient*

What other fruit does the Holy Spirit produce in us? Galatians 5:22 says "longsuffering" is another blessing we can enjoy by habitually living in the Spirit. Let's face it: At times we all get frustrated with someone, and sometimes our level of frustration can rise to the boiling point. It's easy to be nice to people who appreciate us and show us kindness. But what about when people fail to appreciate us — or they're ungrateful for what we do for them? How will we respond when individuals fail to listen to our counsel or fail to value what we have contributed? That's often the moment when our soul says, "Excuse me, but I'm not a doormat for people to wipe their feet on! I've invested all the time and energy I'm willing to invest in this person, and I refuse to help him any further!"

Parents have felt this way toward their children. Teachers have felt this way toward their students. Husbands and wives have felt this way toward their spouses. Friends have felt this way toward their friends, and pastors have felt this way toward their congregations. The bottom line is this: Regardless of your status in life — who you're married to, where you work, or what you do — you need "longsuffering" to successfully get along with other people.

In Galatians 5:22, the apostle Paul lists "longsuffering" as another fruit that the Holy Spirit wants to produce in our lives. This word is a translation of the Greek word *makrothumia*, which is a compound of the words *makros* and *thumos*. The word *makros* means *long* and it is where we get the word "macaroni," which can picture a long noodle before it is cut. And the word *thumos* means *anger* and depicts *a strong and growing passion*. When these words are compounded to form *makrothumia*, it pictures *the patient restraint of anger* and therefore denotes *longsuffering*. This word can also be translated as *forbearance* or *patience*. It is ready to *forbear* and *patiently wait*; it doesn't easily give up or bow out.

The word *makrothumia* — translated here as "longsuffering" — is like a candle that has a very long wick and is prepared to burn a long time. This is a person with the ability to *forbear* and to *patiently wait* until someone finally comes around, makes progress, changes, or hears what you are trying to communicate or teach him or her.

This word *makrothumia* is actually the very word used in First Corinthians 13:4, which says, "Charity [or love] suffereth long...." Other possible interpretive translations of the word *makrothumia* in this verse would be:

- "Love *is not short-tempered* or *easily angered*...."
- "Love *does not quickly blow its top, but it is patient as it waits for others*...."
- "Love *is determined to wait until the other person finally comes around*...."
- "Love *passionately burns for others and is willing to wait as long as necessary*...."
- "Love *is not irritable and impatient, but is willing to wait a long time for someone to change*...."

Indeed, "longsuffering" is very different from the flesh, which gets easily angered, blows up, loses its temper, and says things it later regrets. There is no way we can fake this fruit. If we have it operating in our lives, it will be a supernatural work of the Holy Spirit. If we will cooperate with Him and allow Him to freely work in our lives, we will have the ability to be patient with and tolerant of others just like God is patient with and tolerant of us and all our shortcomings.

'Gentleness' Is the Divine Ability to Be *Adaptable*

In addition to love, joy, peace, and longsuffering, "gentleness" is also included as a fruit of the Spirit (*see* Galatians 5:22). This word "gentleness" comes from the Greek word *chrestotes*, which describes *kindness* or *one who is compassionate, considerate, sympathetic, humane, kind, or gentle*. It conveys the idea of *being adaptable to others*. A person with this trait seeks to become adaptable to the needs of those around him. Rather than demand everyone else to adapt to your own needs and desires, when *chrestotes* is working in you, you will seek to become adaptable to those who are around you.

Paul pointed to this fruit as his motivation for ministry when he wrote to the believers at the church at Corinth. He said:

- "And unto the Jews I became as a Jew, that I might gain the Jews..." (1 Corinthians 9:20).

- "...To them that are under the law, as under the law, that I might gain them..." (1 Corinthians 9:20).

- "...To them that are without law, as without law...that I might gain them..." (1 Corinthians 9:21).

- "To the weak became I as weak, that I might gain the weak..." (1 Corinthians 9:22).

- "...I am made all things to all men, that I might by all means save some" (1 Corinthians 9:22).

Paul was so interested in reaching others and meeting their needs that he was willing to become whatever he needed to be to reach them. He made it one of his aims to walk in *chrestotes*, or in *gentleness* and *kindness*, becoming *adaptable* to others around him so that he could minister to them and meet their needs.

This is so contrary to the flesh! The flesh says, "Excuse me, but if you don't like me the way I am, you can tough it out! This is the way I am, and if you don't like it, you can just get out of here. I'm not changing for anyone!"

But when the Holy Spirit is producing His fruit of gentleness in you, you'll hear yourself thinking and saying, "How can I be different for you? Is there any way I can change that will help you? Is there anything I can do better for you? How can I meet your needs more effectively?"

Friend, it is nothing short of the supernatural work of the Holy Spirit in us when we become *adaptable* to meet the needs of others around us. When we begin seeing *gentleness* — along with the fruit of God's supernatural *joy*, *peace*, and *longsuffering* — operating in our lives, we can know with great confidence that we are indeed habitually living in the Spirit!

STUDY QUESTIONS

Study to shew thyself approved unto God, a workman that needeth not to be ashamed, rightly dividing the word of truth.
— 2 Timothy 2:15

1. *Joy* and *peace* are two powerful fruits of the Spirit that we need Him to develop in our lives. What does God's Word say in these verses we can do to help cultivate these divine virtues?

    • Psalm 16:11 and Isaiah 26:3 _____

    _____

    • Psalm 119:165 and Jeremiah 15:16 _____

    _____

    • Romans 15:13 _____

    _____

    • John 14:27; 16:33; Ephesians 2:14 _____

    _____

    • John 16:24 (along with Matthew 7:7-11) _____

    _____

2. Whether we're dealing with difficult people or difficult situations, peace is often the first thing the enemy tries to steal. What did the Holy Spirit tell us through the apostle Paul in **Philippians 4:6-8** that we are to do *anytime* and *every time* we sense we are losing our peace? Carefully meditate on this powerful passage in a few different Bible translations, and write what the Holy Spirit reveals to you.

PRACTICAL APPLICATION

But be ye doers of the word, and not hearers only, deceiving your own selves.
—James 1:22

1. When you look over your life, can you remember a time when you experienced unexplainable *peace* or supernatural *joy* instead of the worry, frustration, and fear that would normally have gripped your soul? Briefly describe what happened. Do you need God's joy and peace right now? Take a few minutes to pray and ask the Holy Spirit to produce these supernatural fruits in your life.

2. Is there a particular person you seem to have no patience with at all? (Is it *you?*) Do you often lose your cool and say or do things you later regret — things you wouldn't want someone to say or do to you? Pray and ask the Lord, "Why am I having issues with this particular person? What is going on inside of me? Please help me and show me what to do. Thank You, Lord. In Jesus' name, Amen."

3. In what ways might you become more *adaptable* to this person — and others — in order to help that person grow in his or her relationship with God or to help that person receive Jesus as Savior and Lord? Pray and ask the Holy Spirit to develop the fruit of *gentleness* and *longsuffering* in you.

LESSON 10

TOPIC

Goodness, Faith, Meekness, Temperance

SCRIPTURES

1. **Galatians 5:16** — This I say then, Walk in the Spirit, and ye shall not fulfil the lust of the flesh.

2. **Galatians 5:19-21** — Now the works of the flesh are manifest, which are these; Adultery, fornication, uncleanness, lasciviousness, idolatry, witchcraft, hatred, variance, emulations, wrath, strife, seditions, heresies, envyings, murders, drunkenness, revellings, and such like....

3. **Galatians 5:22,23** — But the fruit of the Spirit is love, joy, peace, longsuffering, gentleness, goodness, faith, meekness, temperance; against such there is no law.

4. **Acts 10:38** — How God anointed Jesus of Nazareth with the Holy Ghost and with power: who went about doing good, and healing all that were oppressed of the devil; for God was with him.

5. **Numbers 23:19** (*NIV*) — God is not a man, that he should lie, nor a son of man, that he should change his mind.

6. **Hebrew 13:8** — Jesus Christ, the same yesterday, today, and forever.

GREEK WORDS

1. "this I say" — **Λέγω δέ** (*Lego de*): I say categorically; I say emphatically

2. "walk" — **περιπατέω** (*peripateo*): a compound of the words **περι** (*peri*) and **πατέω** (*pateo*); the word **περι** (*peri*) means *around* and suggests the idea of something that is encircling; the word **πατέω** (*pateo*) means *to walk* and denotes the movement of the feet; when compounded, to habitually walk around in one general vicinity; thus this word **περιπατέω** (*peripateo*) was often translated as the word "live"

3. "shall not" — **οὐ μὴ** (*ou me*): the word **οὐ** (*ou*) is an emphatic *no*; with **μὴ** (*me*), which simply means *no*, it means *you emphatically will not*

4. "goodness" — **ἀγαθωσύνη** (*agathosune*): goodness in the sense of being good to someone; used to portray a person who is generous, big-hearted, liberal, and charitable with his finances; a giver; the act of reaching beyond oneself to meet the natural needs of those around him; pictures philanthropic giving

5. "doing good" — **εὐεργετέω** (*euergeteo*): a benefactor; a philanthropist; one who financially supports charitable works; one who uses his financial resources to meet needs of disadvantaged people; this word was only used in connection with the provision of food, clothes, or some other commodity associated with physical or material needs

6. "faith" — **πίστις** (*pistis*): the most common word for faith in the New Testament; conveys the idea of one who is faithful, reliable, loyal, and steadfast; pictures one who is trustworthy, dependable, dedicated, constant, reliable, dependable, unfailing, and unwavering; it is an unchanging, constant, stable, unwavering belief or behavior

7. "meekness" — **πραΰτης** (*prautes*): a strong-willed person who has learned to bring his strength under control; in rare instances, describes wild animals that were domesticated and brought under control; in a medical sense, denotes soothing medication to calm the angry mind;

one so gentle that he becomes soothing medicine for the angry or upset soul or for a troublesome or unsettling situation

8. "temperance" — ἐγκράτεια (*enkrateia*): from the Greek words ἐν (*en*) and κράτος (*kratos*); the word ἐν (*en*) means in, and the word κράτος (*kratos*) is the Greek word for power; when compounded, power over one's self; hence, it is often translated as self-control; suggests the control or restraint of one's passions, appetites, and desires; restraint, moderation, discipline, balance, temperance, or self-control

SYNOPSIS

When it comes to walking in the Spirit and not fulfilling the lusts of the flesh, few people understood the practice better than the apostle Paul. He learned that in order for the Spirit of God to live in him, his flesh had to "die." This is why he said, "I have been crucified with Christ: and I myself no longer live, but Christ lives in me. And the real life I now have within this body is a result of my trusting in the Son of God, who loved me and gave himself for me" (Galatians 2:20 *TLB*).

Now you may be thinking, *How in the world can I be crucified with Christ? He died more than 2,000 years ago.* Again, we turn to the Holy Spirit-inspired writings of the apostle Paul, where Paul explains:

> **For you have become a part of him [Christ], and so you died with him, so to speak, when he died; and now you share his new life, and shall rise as he did. Your old evil desires were nailed to the cross with him; that part of you that loves to sin was crushed and fatally wounded, so that your sin-loving body is no longer under sin's control, no longer needs to be a slave to sin.**
> **— Romans 6:5,6 (*TLB*)**

This recognition of one's fleshly, old nature being crucified with Christ was an ongoing declaration for Paul. In fact, he said, "…I die *daily* [I face death every day and die to self]" (1 Corinthians 15:31 *AMPC*). So how do we walk and live in the Spirit? We see our carnal nature as crucified with Christ — we are dead to sin and alive to God in Christ Jesus! In this humble position, the fruit of the Spirit will begin to burst forth.

The emphasis of this lesson:

The fruit of *goodness* is a divine desire to give generously, especially to those in need. *Faith* describes faithfulness, reliability, and steadfastness.

When *meekness* is present, it means one has submitted his strong will and attitude to the control of the Spirit. And *temperance* is self-control or restraint of one's passions, appetites, and desires.

A FINAL REVIEW
OF OUR ANCHOR VERSE
Galatians 5:16

Looking at our anchor verse one last time, the apostle Paul said, "This I say then, Walk in the Spirit, and ye shall not fulfill the lust of the flesh" (Galatians 5:16). When Paul wrote, "This I say," he used the Greek words *Lego de*. The word *Lego* means *I say*, which is very strong by itself, but it becomes even stronger when he adds the intensifying word *de*, which describes something that is *absolute*, *categorical*, or *emphatic*. When these words are put together, it's the equivalent of Paul raising his voice and saying:

> "Now hear me! Hear what I'm saying to you! I'm going to tell you something that is unquestionable, indisputable, and absolutely certain...."

What did Paul so confidently say we could count on being true? He said, "...Walk in the Spirit, and ye shall not fulfill the lust of the flesh" (Galatians 5:16). Once more, this word "walk" is the Greek word *peripateo*, which is a compound of the words *peri* and *pateo*. The word *peri* means *around* and describes something that is *encircling*. And the word *pateo* comes from the Greek word meaning *to walk*. When these words are compounded to form the word *peripateo*, it depicts *one who habitually walks around in one general vicinity all the time*. In no way does this describe a haphazard or accidental visit — nor is it a once a week achievement on Sundays to be spiritual. On the contrary, the word *peripateo* depicts one who has walked and walked in one realm for so long it has become their place of existence. Therefore, we could translate this part of the verse:

> "This I say to you emphatically, categorically, and with absolute certainty. If you habitually and continually walk and live in the Spirit, you shall not fulfill the lust of the flesh."

Again, the words "shall not" in Greek are *ou mé*. The word *ou* is an emphatic *no*, and the word *mé* also means *no*. Together, they form a double negative that literally means, *"You absolutely and emphatically will not, in any way, fulfill the lust of the flesh."* To walk in the Spirit and defeat the flesh, you must consistently say *yes* to the Spirit and say *no* to the flesh — denying the flesh the opportunity to operate. If you will step up onto this high road of righteousness and begin to live in the realm of the Spirit, you will effectively pull the plug on the flesh.

Taking into account the original Greek meaning of the key words in this verse, here is the *Renner Interpretive Version* (*RIV*) of Galatians 5:16:

> **Make the path of the Spirit the place where you habitually live and walk. Become so comfortable on this spiritual path that you learn to leisurely and peacefully stroll along in that realm. Living your life in this Spirit realm is the best way to guarantee that you will not allow the yearnings of your flesh to creep out and fulfill themselves.**

What will your flesh do if you let it run your life? Very candidly, the apostle Paul tells us, "Now the works of the flesh are manifest, which are these; Adultery, fornication, uncleanness, lasciviousness, idolatry, witchcraft, hatred, variance, emulations, wrath, strife, seditions, heresies, envyings, murders, drunkenness, revellings, and such like…" (Galatians 5:19-21).

In contrast, when you let the Holy Spirit lead your life, you can expect Him to produce His fruit in you. Galatians 5:22 and 23 says, "But the fruit of the Spirit is love, joy, peace, longsuffering, gentleness, goodness, faith, meekness, temperance; against such there is no law."

'Goodness' Is a Divine Desire To *Give Generously*

In Galatians 5:22, the apostle Paul includes "goodness" as one of the fruit of the Spirit. This word "goodness" is the Greek word *agathosune*, which means *goodness* in the sense of *being good to someone*. This word was used to portray *a person who is generous, big-hearted, liberal, and charitable with his finances*. We would call this person *a giver*. Furthermore, "goodness" (*agathosune*) is *the act of reaching beyond oneself to meet the natural needs of those around him*. It is a picture of *philanthropic giving*.

What you may not know is this type of giving was on display in the ministry of Jesus, and Acts 10:38 confirms it. The Bible says, "How God anointed Jesus of Nazareth with the Holy Ghost and with power: who went about doing good, and healing all that were oppressed of the devil; for God was with him."

Notice the words "doing good." They are from the old Greek word *euergeteo*, which denoted *a benefactor, a philanthropist, one who financially supports charitable works,* or *one who uses his financial resources to meet needs of disadvantaged people.* This word was only used in connection with the provision of food, clothes, or some other commodity associated with physical or material needs.

This tells us Jesus didn't only perform supernatural works; He also used His resources to do good works in the natural realm. That is, Jesus cared for the poor. He helped feed the needy and utilized the vast resources and finances made available to His ministry to meet the basic needs of human beings. This explains why Jesus needed a treasurer for His ministry. It also lets us know that acting in "goodness" is the nature of God. He is a *benefactor,* a *philanthropist,* and one that is concerned with meeting the practical needs of those in need.

So when the Bible tells us that one of the fruits of the Spirit is "goodness," it lets us know God wants us to be selfless, using our resources to help change people's living conditions for the better. This is absolutely contrary to the flesh, which consumes every spare dollar on itself. But when the Spirit is working mightily in us, He shifts our focus from ourselves to the needs of those who are around us. Thus, the fruit of "goodness" is *a Spirit-produced urge to reach beyond oneself to meet the natural needs of those around him.* The truth is, there should be no greater *benefactor* or *philanthropist* than a person filled with the Spirit!

'Faith' Is *Faithfulness, Reliability,* and *Steadfastness*

Along with goodness, the Holy Spirit produces the fruit of "faith" in us. This word "faith" is the Greek word *pistis,* the most common word for *faith* in the New Testament. It conveys the idea of *one who is faithful, reliable, loyal, and steadfast.* It pictures *one who is trustworthy, dependable, dedicated, constant, reliable, dependable, unfailing, and unwavering.* Moreover, it is *an unchanging, constant, stable, unwavering belief or behavior.*

This is so contrary to the flesh, which is naturally lazy, uncommitted, undependable, and unreliable. But this fruit of the Spirit — which is often translated as "faithfulness" — is a part of the eternal nature of God. So it makes sense that if the divine Seed of God is in you, the Spirit of God will begin to produce faithfulness (*faith*) in your life. First Corinthians 1:9 says, "God is faithful...." We read about this being His character in Numbers 23:19 (*NIV*), which says, "God is not a man, that he should lie, nor a son of man, that he should change his mind."

In other words, what God says He is going to do is what He does. He is *stable* and *unchanging*. This truth is confirmed in Hebrews 13:8 (*NKJV*), which declares, "Jesus Christ is the same yesterday, today, and forever."

Again, since this unchanging, constant, stable, unwavering behavior is the nature of God — and His Seed is inside you — it shouldn't surprise you that when His Spirit is allowed to work in you, He makes you faithful and steadfast, just like God! God is faithful, and, therefore, faithfulness should grow in our lives as one of the fruits of the Holy Spirit.

'Meekness' Is Not Weakness — It Is *Strength Under Control*

The apostle Paul opens Galatians 5:23 by adding "meekness" to the list of the fruit of the Spirit. Although many have equated "meekness" with weakness, that is incorrect. The word "meekness" is the Greek word *prautes*, and it actually depicts *a strong-willed person who has learned to bring his strength under control*. This denotes *one who is patient and slow to respond in anger, one who remains in control of himself even in the face of insults or injuries.*

Again, one who is "meek" isn't weak — he is *controlled*. He may possess a strong will and a strong character and may have his own strong opinions. But this person has learned the secret of submitting to those who are over him. Thus, he knows how to *bring his will and conduct under control.* In rare instances, this word described wild animals that were domesticated and brought under control.

So when the Holy Spirit is producing meekness in your life, you can be controlled even in difficult circumstances. Rather than fly into a rage and throw a temper tantrum, you are able to remain silent and keep your emotions and temper under control. If you find yourself in a hard situation that you fiercely believe is wrong, you are still able to stay silent until the appropriate moment to speak or until you have been asked for your opinion. You know how to control yourself and your emotions.

In addition to these meanings, the word "meekness" was also used in a medical sense to denote *soothing medication to calm the angry mind*. A meek person doesn't project the demeanor of one who is offended, upset, angry, or reactive to insults or injuries. Instead, he has learned to *control himself* and be so *gentle* in his response that he becomes *soothing medicine* for the angry or upset people, or for a troublesome and unsettling situation.

This is quite contrary to the flesh, which loves to rage out of control. But when meekness is being produced in you by the Holy Spirit, it will make you careful and controlled. Your very presence can become God's soothing medication for angry, upset people.

'Temperance' Is Supernatural *Self-Control*

Rounding out the nine fruits of the Spirit is the fruit of "temperance." In Greek, this is the word *enkrateia*, from the Greek words *en* and *kratos*. The word *en* means *in*, and the word *kratos* is the Greek word for *power*. When these words are compounded, the new word *enkrateia* means *in control* and denotes *power over one's self*. Hence, it is often translated as *self-control*, especially in newer English translations. This word suggests *the control or restraint of one's passions, appetites, and desires*.

Just as a meek person can control his attitude, an individual with temperance has power over his appetites, physical urges, passions, and desires. Through the power of the Holy Spirit, he is able to say no to overeating, no to overindulging in fleshly activities, and no to *any* excesses in the physical realm. A person with temperance maintains a life of *moderation* and *control*. The word *enkrateia* — translated as "temperance" — could be translated as *restraint, moderation, discipline, balance, temperance*, or *self-control*.

You can see how opposite temperance is to the works of the flesh. If the flesh is allowed to have its way it will OVERDO it every time. It will over-worry, over-work, over-eat, over-indulge, and run itself to death. But when a person is controlled by the Holy Spirit, God's Spirit produces in him a discipline over the physical realm that helps him sustain his physical condition, stay in good health, remain free from sin, and live a life that is moderate and balanced.

Now that you better understand the meanings of "temperance" and "meekness," can *you* control your temper and your physical appetites and urges?

Are you able to restrain your emotions and keep your flesh under control? Or would you have to honestly say that your flesh is running the show?

Don't allow your flesh to run your life! In the words of the apostle Paul, "Let us be Christ's men [and women] from head to foot, and give no chances to the flesh to have its fling" (Romans 13:14 *J. B. Phillips*). Likewise, "This I say then, Walk in the Spirit, and ye shall not fulfil the lust of the flesh" (Galatians 5:16).

Taking into account the original Greek meaning of the key words in this verse, here again is the *Renner Interpretive Version* (*RIV*) of Galatians 5:16:

> **Make the path of the Spirit the place where you habitually live and walk. Become so comfortable on this spiritual path that you learn to leisurely and peacefully stroll along in that realm. Living your life in this Spirit realm is the best way to guarantee that you will not allow the yearnings of your flesh to creep out and fulfill themselves.**

As we close this series, hear this charge from the apostle Paul as if he was standing right in front of you speaking to you personally: "Therefore, dear brothers and sisters, you have no obligation to do what your sinful nature urges you to do. For if you live by its dictates, you will die. But if **through the power of the Spirit** you put to death the deeds of your sinful nature, you will live. For all who are led by the Spirit of God are children of God" (Romans 8:12-14 *NLT*). Crush the cravings of your flesh and walk in the Spirit! Ask Him for the power to keep your old sinful nature nailed to the Cross every day, and you will begin to experience life like you've never imagined!

STUDY QUESTIONS

> **Study to shew thyself approved unto God, a workman that needeth not to be ashamed, rightly dividing the word of truth.**
> **— 2 Timothy 2:15**

1. A major key to walking in the Spirit is to *"starve your flesh."* What you feed is going to live, and what you starve is going to die. Stop and take an honest inventory of what you regularly feed your soul and spirit. What websites are your surfing? What TV shows and movies are you watching? What video games are you playing? What do you know

you need to cut from your media menu in order to starve your flesh? And how important is feeding on God's Word? (Meditate on 2 Timothy 3:15-17; Psalm 119:9; John 17:17; Ephesians 5:26; Joshua 1:8.)

2. Do you want to care for the poor and help feed the needy like Jesus did? You can! Read Second Corinthians 9:6-13 and see how God promises to provide for you — and all the blessings that result from being generous. Then pray for the Holy Spirit to supernaturally open your eyes to see the needs of those around you that He has equipped you to help.

3. The rewards of being *faithful* and *steadfast* are literally out of this world! Consider what God's Word says in First Corinthians 15:58; Galatians 6:7-9; Colossians 3:23,24; and James 1:12.

PRACTICAL APPLICATION

**But be ye doers of the word, and not hearers only,
deceiving your own selves.**
— James 1:22

1. Of all nine of the fruits of the Spirit — love, joy, peace, longsuffering, gentleness, goodness, faith, meekness, and temperance — which ones can you clearly see are growing in your life? What evidence can you point to that verifies this?

2. When it comes to dealing with difficult people and challenging situations, would you say you have a *calming* effect or an *irritating, frustrating* effect on people? What if we were to ask those who know you best? Would they say you're like *soothing medicine* for the angry, upset soul, or like gasoline on a fire? How do you usually respond to insults, injuries, and volatile situations?

3. Be honest. In what areas of your life does your flesh seem to dominate you and you need greater control (meekness and temperance)? Take time to pray: "Lord, I ask You to forgive me for allowing my flesh to run the show in these areas of my life: _____. Please wash me clean of any and all sin and begin to cultivate the fruit of meekness and self-control in me. Thank You, Lord, for Your patience and for empowering me to do what I cannot do on my own. In Jesus' name, amen."